The Department of Commerce

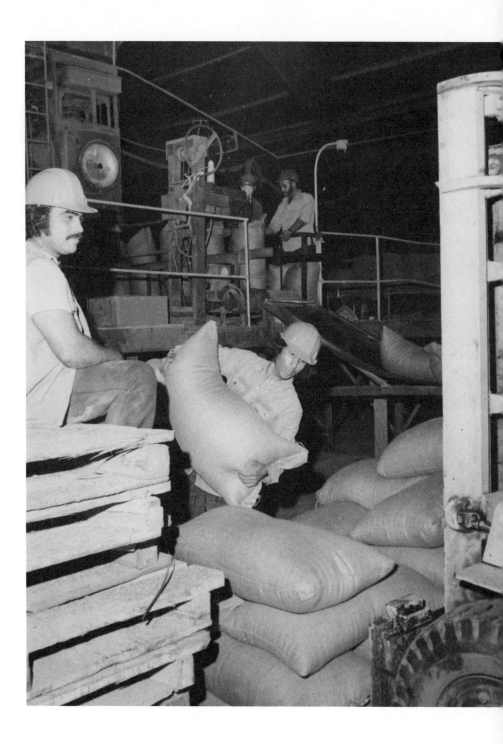

KNOW YOUR GOVERNMENT

The Department of Commerce

Robert J. Griffin, Jr.

CHELSEA HOUSE PUBLISHERS

On the cover: *Left:* A 1990 census enumerator visits a family who did not respond to the census questionnaire. *Top right:* Scientists at the National Hurricane Center keep track of a potentially dangerous storm. *Bottom right:* Freight containers are loaded for overseas shipment at Port Elizabeth, New Jersey.
Frontispiece: Workers load bags of wheat for shipment to the People's Democratic Republic of Yemen.

Chelsea House Publishers
Editor-in-Chief: Remmel Nunn
Managing Editor: Karyn Gullen Browne
Copy Chief: Juliann Barbato
Picture Editor: Adrian G. Allen
Art Director: Maria Epes
Deputy Copy Chief: Mark Rifkin
Assistant Art Director: Loraine Machlin
Manufacturing Manager: Gerald Levine
Systems Manager: Rachel Vigier
Production Manager: Joseph Romano
Production Coordinator: Marie Claire Cebrián

Know Your Government
Senior Editor: Kathy Kuhtz

Staff for THE DEPARTMENT OF COMMERCE
Associate Editor: Scott Prentzas
Copy Editor: Michael Goodman
Picture Research: Dixon & Turner Research Associates, Inc.
Picture Coordinator: Melanie Sanford
Senior Designer: Noreen Romano

First Printing

1 3 5 7 9 8 6 4 2

Library of Congress Cataloging-in-Publication Data

Griffin, Robert J., Jr.
   The Department of Commerce/Robert J. Griffin, Jr.
      p.   cm.—(Know your government)
   Includes bibliographical references.
   ISBN 0-87754-836-6
         0-7910-0885-1 (pbk.)
      1. United States. Dept. of Commerce—History.   2. Executive
departments—United States—History.   I. Title.   II. Series: Know
your government (New York, N.Y.)
HF73.U5G75   1990   90-1481
353.82—dc20   CIP

CONTENTS

KNOW YOUR GOVERNMENT

CHELSEA HOUSE PUBLISHERS

INTRODUCTION

Government: Crises of Confidence

Arthur M. Schlesinger, jr.

From the start, Americans have regarded their government with a mixture of reliance and mistrust. The men who founded the republic did not doubt the indispensability of government. "If men were angels," observed the 51st Federalist Paper, "no government would be necessary." But men are not angels. Because human beings are subject to wicked as well as to noble impulses, government was deemed essential to assure freedom and order.

At the same time, the American revolutionaries knew that government could also become a source of injury and oppression. The men who gathered in Philadelphia in 1787 to write the Constitution therefore had two purposes in mind. They wanted to establish a strong central authority and to limit that central authority's capacity to abuse its power.

To prevent the abuse of power, the Founding Fathers wrote two basic principles into the new Constitution. The principle of federalism divided power between the state governments and the central authority. The principle of the separation of powers subdivided the central authority itself into three branches— the executive, the legislative, and the judiciary—so that "each may be a check on the other." The *Know Your Government* series focuses on the major executive departments and agencies in these branches of the federal government.

The Constitution did not plan the executive branch in any detail. After vesting the executive power in the president, it assumed the existence of "executive departments" without specifying what these departments should be. Congress began defining their functions in 1789 by creating the Departments of State, Treasury, and War. The secretaries in charge of these departments made up President Washington's first cabinet. Congress also provided for a legal officer, and President Washington soon invited the attorney general, as he was called, to attend cabinet meetings. As need required, Congress created more executive departments.

Setting up the cabinet was only the first step in organizing the American state. With almost no guidance from the Constitution, President Washington, seconded by Alexander Hamilton, his brilliant secretary of the treasury, equipped the infant republic with a working administrative structure. The Federalists believed in both executive energy and executive accountability and set high standards for public appointments. The Jeffersonian opposition had less faith in strong government and preferred local government to the central authority. But when Jefferson himself became president in 1801, although he set out to change the direction of policy, he found no reason to alter the framework the Federalists had erected.

By 1801 there were about 3,000 federal civilian employees in a nation of a little more than 5 million people. Growth in territory and population steadily enlarged national responsibilities. Thirty years later, when Jackson was president, there were more than 11,000 government workers in a nation of 13 million. The federal establishment was increasing at a faster rate than the population.

Jackson's presidency brought significant changes in the federal service. He believed that the executive branch contained too many officials who saw their jobs as "species of property" and as "a means of promoting individual interest." Against the idea of a permanent service based on life tenure, Jackson argued for the periodic redistribution of federal offices, contending that this was the democratic way and that official duties could be made "so plain and simple that men of intelligence may readily qualify themselves for their performance." He called this policy rotation-in-office. His opponents called it the spoils system.

In fact, partisan legend exaggerated the extent of Jackson's removals. More than 80 percent of federal officeholders retained their jobs. Jackson discharged no larger a proportion of government workers than Jefferson had done a generation earlier. But the rise in these years of mass political parties gave federal patronage new importance as a means of building the party and of rewarding activists. Jackson's successors were less restrained in the distribu-

8

tion of spoils. As the federal establishment grew—to nearly 40,000 by 1861—the politicization of the public service excited increasing concern.

After the Civil War the spoils system became a major political issue. High-minded men condemned it as the root of all political evil. The spoilsmen, said the British commentator James Bryce, "have distorted and depraved the mechanism of politics." Patronage, by giving jobs to unqualified, incompetent, and dishonest persons, lowered the standards of public service and nourished corrupt political machines. Office-seekers pursued presidents and cabinet secretaries without mercy. "Patronage," said Ulysses S. Grant after his presidency, "is the bane of the presidential office." "Every time I appoint someone to office," said another political leader, "I make a hundred enemies and one ingrate." George William Curtis, the president of the National Civil Service Reform League, summed up the indictment. He said,

> The theory which perverts public trusts into party spoils, making public
> employment dependent upon personal favor and not on proved merit,
> necessarily ruins the self-respect of public employees, destroys the
> function of party in a republic, prostitutes elections into a desperate
> strife for personal profit, and degrades the national character by lower-
> ing the moral tone and standard of the country.

The object of civil service reform was to promote efficiency and honesty in the public service and to bring about the ethical regeneration of public life. Over bitter opposition from politicians, the reformers in 1883 passed the Pendleton Act, establishing a bipartisan Civil Service Commission, competitive examinations, and appointment on merit. The Pendleton Act also gave the president authority to extend by executive order the number of "classified" jobs—that is, jobs subject to the merit system. The act applied initially only to about 14,000 of the more than 100,000 federal positions. But by the end of the 19th century 40 percent of federal jobs had moved into the classified category.

Civil service reform was in part a response to the growing complexity of American life. As society grew more organized and problems more technical, official duties were no longer so plain and simple that any person of intelligence could perform them. In public service, as in other areas, the all-round man was yielding ground to the expert, the amateur to the professional. The excesses of the spoils system thus provoked the counter-ideal of scientific public administration, separate from politics and, as far as possible, insulated against it.

The cult of the expert, however, had its own excesses. The idea that administration could be divorced from policy was an illusion. And in the realm of policy, the expert, however much segregated from partisan politics, can never attain perfect objectivity. He remains the prisoner of his own set of values. It is these values rather than technical expertise that determine fundamental judgments of public policy. To turn over such judgments to experts, moreover, would be to abandon democracy itself; for in a democracy final decisions must be made by the people and their elected representatives. "The business of the expert," the British political scientist Harold Laski rightly said, "is to be on tap and not on top."

Politics, however, were deeply ingrained in American folkways. This meant intermittent tension between the presidential government, elected every four years by the people, and the permanent government, which saw presidents come and go while it went on forever. Sometimes the permanent government knew better than its political masters; sometimes it opposed or sabotaged valuable new initiatives. In the end a strong president with effective cabinet secretaries could make the permanent government responsive to presidential purpose, but it was often an exasperating struggle.

The struggle within the executive branch was less important, however, than the growing impatience with bureaucracy in society as a whole. The 20th century saw a considerable expansion of the federal establishment. The Great Depression and the New Deal led the national government to take on a variety of new responsibilities. The New Deal extended the federal regulatory apparatus. By 1940, in a nation of 130 million people, the number of federal workers for the first time passed the 1 million mark. The Second World War brought federal civilian employment to 3.8 million in 1945. With peace, the federal establishment declined to around 2 million by 1950. Then growth resumed, reaching 2.8 million by the 1980s.

The New Deal years saw rising criticism of "big government" and "bureaucracy." Businessmen resented federal regulation. Conservatives worried about the impact of paternalistic government on individual self-reliance, on community responsibility, and on economic and personal freedom. The nation in effect renewed the old debate between Hamilton and Jefferson in the early republic, although with an ironic exchange of positions. For the Hamiltonian constituency, the "rich and well-born," once the advocate of affirmative government, now condemned government intervention, while the Jeffersonian constituency, the plain people, once the advocate of a weak central government and of states' rights, now favored government intervention.

In the 1980s, with the presidency of Ronald Reagan, the debate has burst out with unusual intensity. According to conservatives, government intervention abridges liberty, stifles enterprise, and is inefficient, wasteful, and arbitrary. It disturbs the harmony of the self-adjusting market and creates worse troubles than it solves. Get government off our backs, according to the popular cliché, and our problems will solve themselves. When government is necessary, let it be at the local level, close to the people. Above all, stop the inexorable growth of the federal government.

In fact, for all the talk about the "swollen" and "bloated" bureaucracy, the federal establishment has not been growing as inexorably as many Americans seem to believe. In 1949, it consisted of 2.1 million people. Thirty years later, while the country had grown by 70 million, the federal force had grown only by 750,000. Federal workers were a smaller percentage of the population in 1985 than they were in 1955—or in 1940. The federal establishment, in short, has not kept pace with population growth. Moreover, national defense and the postal service account for 60 percent of federal employment.

Why then the widespread idea about the remorseless growth of government? It is partly because in the 1960s the national government assumed new and intrusive functions: affirmative action in civil rights, environmental protection, safety and health in the workplace, community organization, legal aid to the poor. Although this enlargement of the federal regulatory role was accompanied by marked growth in the size of government on all levels, the expansion has taken place primarily in state and local government. Whereas the federal force increased by only 27 percent in the 30 years after 1950, the state and local government force increased by an astonishing 212 percent.

Despite the statistics, the conviction flourishes in some minds that the national government is a steadily growing behemoth swallowing up the liberties of the people. The foes of Washington prefer local government, feeling it is closer to the people and therefore allegedly more responsive to popular needs. Obviously there is a great deal to be said for settling local questions locally. But local government is characteristically the government of the locally powerful. Historically, the way the locally powerless have won their human and constitutional rights has often been through appeal to the national government. The national government has vindicated racial justice against local bigotry, defended the Bill of Rights against local vigilantism, and protected natural resources against local greed. It has civilized industry and secured the rights of labor organizations. Had the states' rights creed prevailed, there would perhaps still be slavery in the United States.

The national authority, far from diminishing the individual, has given most Americans more personal dignity and liberty than ever before. The individual freedoms destroyed by the increase in national authority have been in the main

11

the freedom to deny black Americans their rights as citizens; the freedom to put small children to work in mills and immigrants in sweatshops; the freedom to pay starvation wages, require barbarous working hours, and permit squalid working conditions; the freedom to deceive in the sale of goods and securities; the freedom to pollute the environment—all freedoms that, one supposes, a civilized nation can readily do without.

"Statements are made," said President John F. Kennedy in 1963, "labelling the Federal Government an outsider, an intruder, an adversary. . . . The United States Government is not a stranger or not an enemy. It is the people of fifty states joining in a national effort. . . . Only a great national effort by a great people working together can explore the mysteries of space, harvest the products at the bottom of the ocean, and mobilize the human, natural, and material resources of our lands."

So an old debate continues. However, Americans are of two minds. When pollsters ask large, spacious questions—Do you think government has become too involved in your lives? Do you think government should stop regulating business?—a sizable majority opposes big government. But when asked specific questions about the practical work of government—Do you favor social security? unemployment compensation? Medicare? health and safety standards in factories? environmental protection? government guarantee of jobs for everyone seeking employment? price and wage controls when inflation threatens?—a sizable majority approves of intervention.

In general, Americans do not want less government. What they want is more efficient government. They want government to do a better job. For a time in the 1970s, with Vietnam and Watergate, Americans lost confidence in the national government. In 1964, more than three-quarters of those polled had thought the national government could be trusted to do right most of the time. By 1980 only one-quarter was prepared to offer such trust. But by 1984 trust in the federal government to manage national affairs had climbed back to 45 percent.

Bureaucracy is a term of abuse. But it is impossible to run any large organization, whether public or private, without a bureaucracy's division of labor and hierarchy of authority. And we live in a world of large organizations. Without bureaucracy modern society would collapse. The problem is not to abolish bureaucracy, but to make it flexible, efficient, and capable of innovation.

Two hundred years after the drafting of the Constitution, Americans still regard government with a mixture of reliance and mistrust—a good combination. Mistrust is the best way to keep government reliable. Informed criticism is the means of correcting governmental inefficiency, incompetence, and arbitrariness; that is, of best enabling government to play its essential role. For without government, we cannot attain the goals of the Founding Fathers. Without an understanding of government, we cannot have the informed criticism that makes government do the job right. It is the duty of every American citizen to know our government—which is what this series is all about.

From the bow of a Soviet grain ship, a Houston, Texas, longshoreman supervises the loading of 148 million bushels of wheat. To promote the general welfare, the Department of Commerce helps U.S. businesses develop overseas markets for their products and services.

ONE

To Promote the General Welfare

Although the Department of Commerce was not established until early in the 20th century, its origins and many of the programs that it directs are nearly as old as the United States itself. At the time of the department's founding in 1913, its central mission was, as it remains today, the promotion of American trade and industry at home and the improvement of U.S. business competitiveness in world markets.

The major goals of government, as viewed by the founding fathers, were explicitly stated in the preamble to the Constitution:

> We, the people of the United States, in order to form a more perfect Union, establish justice, insure domestic tranquillity, provide for the common defense, promote the general welfare, and secure the blessings of liberty to ourselves and our posterity, do ordain and establish this Constitution for the United States of America.

One way for the federal government to "promote the general welfare" is for it to encourage and enhance commerce. And, indeed, it was for this very purpose—to enhance commerce by removing the trade barriers that were restricting interstate commerce among the 13 newly independent states—that some of the nation's leading statesmen and citizens assembled in Philadelphia in May 1787. The delegates to the Constitutional Convention, however, did not limit their deliberations to matters of trade and commerce but expanded their work to create a wholly new constitutional form of government to strengthen the politically disunited and economically unstable young nation.

In the 126 years between the signing of the Constitution and the founding of the Department of Commerce in 1913, the federal government assumed many responsibilities to carry out its duty to foster trade and commerce. To facilitate commercial navigation, Congress authorized federal maintenance of lighthouses in 1789. The Patent Office was established in 1836 to protect the interests of inventors and to encourage creativity. Later, the Steamboat Inspection Service was created to guarantee the safety of waterborne commerce and facilitate interstate transportation of goods and people. In 1870, Congress created the General Weather Service, which provided weather information to the public. These agencies, along with other functions performed by the federal government, became important building blocks for the Department of Commerce.

A lighthouse on the rocky coast of Maine alerts ships that they are approaching land. Among its early efforts to foster trade and commerce, Congress authorized the federal maintenance of lighthouses in 1789.

A ship goes through a set of locks to reach a higher water level at the Panama Canal, which allows passage from the Atlantic Ocean to the Pacific Ocean. The United States constructed the canal, which opened to commercial traffic in 1914, signaling its emergence as a major power in international trade.

Spurred by President Theodore Roosevelt and business leaders, Congress passed legislation that created the Department of Commerce and Labor in February 1903. After it became apparent that the same department could not be expected to represent the conflicting interests of business and labor, President William Howard Taft signed legislation on March 4, 1913, that split the Department of Commerce and Labor into two separate cabinet-level departments. The United States finally had a government agency devoted entirely to promoting and developing the nation's industry and trade.

By the time of the founding of the Department of Commerce, the United States had emerged from the Industrial Revolution as a major force in the world economy. Millions of Americans had left the farms and rural areas, moving to the rapidly growing cities. There, along with several million immigrants, they worked in factories to create all sorts of new and hitherto unimagined products—goods and materials that would forever transform life in the United States. Structural steel made it possible for engineers and architects to span great rivers and build soaring skyscrapers. Automobiles broke through the

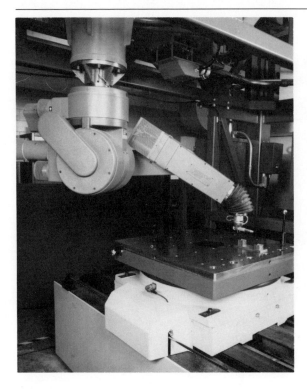

In an experiment at a National Institute of Standards and Technology (NIST) laboratory, an industrial robot holds a machine part while it is tested for flaws. By aiding in the development of industrial robots and conducting research in automated manufacturing processes, NIST helps U.S. businesses become more efficient and competitive.

barriers of distance, permitting people to live, work, and shop with relative ease over vastly greater geographic areas. Telephones enabled the human voice to communicate instantly across the continent and even across the oceans. Electric lights extended work and leisure hours. And a cornucopia of newly invented machines increased productivity in the home and workplace.

The founding of the Department of Commerce thus coincided with some of the most exciting and innovative times in American history. The Panama Canal, which opened in 1914, symbolized America's growing importance in worldwide trade and commerce. Oscar S. Straus, secretary of commerce and labor (1906–1909), captured the spirit of the times:

> Our age has been properly called an era of commercial expansion, and the United States, by reason of its many exceptional advantages, its boundless natural resources, and possessing a growing, intelligent, energetic, enterprising and self-reliant population, is reaping a greater share of industrial and commercial prosperity than any of the other nations of the world.

The Department of Commerce, throughout its history, has helped American business expand, innovate, and bring the advantages of material goods and prosperity to increasing numbers of Americans. The Department of Commerce has grown from an initial budget of $123,600 and a staff of 10,125 in 1914 to an annual budget of nearly $2.5 billion and a staff of more than 52,000 in 1988. Commerce employees are engaged in a wide variety of important and interesting activities: predicting the weather, performing undersea research, taking the census, promoting the sale of U.S. aerospace products, encouraging foreign tourists to spend their vacations in the United States, and assisting industry in developing technologies in such fields as automation, electronics, advanced-materials science, biotechnology, and optics.

The story of the Department of Commerce is intimately bound up with the story of material progress and change in the United States. In 1790, the United States was an undeveloped nation of approximately 4 million people, living together in a weak confederation of 13 coastal states. Four-fifths of the labor force were farmers, and technology and finished goods came mostly from abroad. Today, the United States spans the North American continent and has a population of nearly 250 million people who live in an affluent, industrial society. By fostering economic opportunities and encouraging the increased applications of science and technology in the development of U.S. industrial capacity, the Department of Commerce seeks to fulfill its mandate to promote the general welfare of the citizens of the United States.

A New York sawmill in the 1780s produces lumber. Until the emergence of the railroad, textile, and steel industries in the mid-19th century, commerce in the United States was based primarily on agriculture and shipping.

TWO

Commerce in the New Nation

Following their victory in the revolutionary war, the former 13 colonies—now states under the loose-knit Articles of Confederation and Perpetual Union that each had ratified by 1781—turned their energies to building a new nation and establishing a strong economy. The path that led the group of newly independent states from the pursuit of their own interests to true political unity would prove difficult. Under the Articles of Confederation, the national government consisted of a single legislative body—Congress—in which each state, regardless of its population, had one vote. Because it could not collect taxes or establish a national currency, Congress could only raise money by asking the states for it and could not force an unwilling state to pay its share. The articles also did not provide for an executive or a judiciary branch.

On the other hand, the articles granted the state governments many powers. Each state was free to create its own currency, to develop commercial regulations and levy tariffs (a charge imposed by a government on imported goods), and to tax neighboring states for the use of its ports, roads, and waterways employed in interstate or foreign commerce.

The national economy, which Congress had little power to regulate, teetered on the brink of disaster. The former colonies, which had been united in war, began bickering among themselves and pursuing their own local interests to the detriment of the general welfare of the nation. The disparity of laws from state to state caused endless confusion for businesses conducting interstate commerce, and the states inhibited trade among themselves by levying tariffs against the goods of other states. In addition, the fledgling nation's credit was poor because it had not paid its war debts. The federal government owed back pay to soldiers and faced repayment of the money that it had borrowed from other countries to support the war effort. As a result, European financiers were reluctant to lend money to the U.S. government. If these problems had been allowed to fester indefinitely, the United States might have remained a collection of separate, jealous, and continually quarreling states.

Fortunately, such leading statesmen as George Washington, James Madison, and Alexander Hamilton recognized the inherent weaknesses of the Articles of Confederation and moved with increasing decisiveness to achieve a workable remedy: a truly united, yet federal, republic. They envisioned a nation composed of individual states that were bound by common laws and institutions.

Forming an Effective Federal Government

In 1785, George Washington, who was interested in extending transportation on the Potomac River from the Atlantic Ocean all the way to the Ohio Valley, invited legislators from Virginia and Maryland to meet at his Mount Vernon home to settle differences that had arisen over navigation rights on the river, which separates the two states. At the Mount Vernon Conference, as the meeting became known, the delegates drafted a 13-point agreement that covered commercial regulations, fishing and navigational rights, toll duties, and rules for debt collection. The agreement was designed to ensure mutually profitable commerce on all waterways of the Potomac.

The success of the Mount Vernon Conference encouraged James Madison, who headed the committee in the Virginia legislature that received the conference's report, to propose a resolution calling for all of the states to send representatives to a convention to discuss and resolve the commercial problems created by tariffs and other barriers to interstate commerce. In September 1786, representatives from five states—Delaware, New Jersey, New York, Pennsylvania, and Virginia (the other states did not send delegations)—met in Annapolis, Maryland, to discuss the issues surrounding trade and commerce in the United States. The members of the five-state convention quickly realized that to be truly effective all of the states must address their common trade problems jointly. Madison and Alexander Hamilton

George Washington oversees farm work at his Mount Vernon estate in Virginia. In 1785, Washington invited legislators from Virginia and Maryland to Mount Vernon to discuss navigation rights on the Potomac River. Some of the commercial and political issues discussed at the Mount Vernon Conference resurfaced two years later at the Constitutional Convention.

of New York also convinced the delegates that a more important question was at issue—the inadequacy of the federal government created by the Articles of Confederation.

Hamilton, in a proposal endorsed by James Madison and Edmund Randolph of Virginia, called for a third meeting, to be attended by representatives from all 13 states, that would consider drafting a constitution for a federal government that would be strong enough to fulfill the needs and meet the challenges of the nation. Hamilton sent his proposal to the members of Congress and the governors of all the states. The proposal was largely ignored until the end of 1786, when a band of Massachusetts farmers tried to prevent the state courts from foreclosing the mortgages on their farms. They marched to Springfield, the state capital, to get weapons from an arsenal, but were defeated by the state militia. The uprising, known as Shays's Rebellion (named after the group's leader, Daniel Shays), frightened many prominent statesmen and wealthy citizens. Public opinion quickly shifted in favor of a new and stronger federal government that would be able to unify the nation, prevent mob rule, and coordinate the national economy.

The third meeting, known as the Constitutional Convention, was held in Philadelphia from May to September 1787 and presided over by George Washington. The delegates soon acknowledged the inherent weaknesses of the Articles of Confederation, not only with respect to matters of trade but in other areas of national life as well. They chose to cast aside the articles and to write an entirely new constitution, creating a more powerful and effective central government. The new constitution established a federal system composed of three equal and independent branches—the executive, legislative, and judiciary. It also granted express power to the federal government to "regulate commerce with foreign nations and among the several states."

A delegate from New Jersey, Gouverneur Morris, proposed that the Constitution establish a "Council of State" to direct the affairs of the new national government. A secretary of commerce and finance, who would be

The delegates to the Constitutional Convention in 1787 debate a proposal during their efforts to restructure the federal government. Removing trade barriers between the states to improve the economy of the nation was among the goals of the framers of the Constitution.

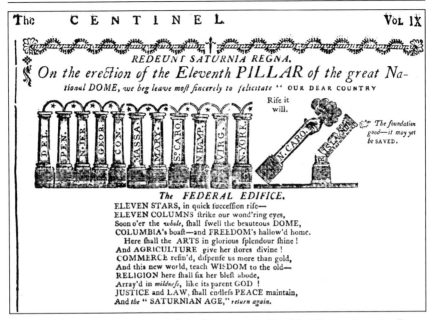

The CENTINEL. Vol IX

REDEUNT SATURNIA REGNA.

On the erection of the Eleventh PILLAR of the great National DOME, we beg leave most sincerely to felicitate "OUR DEAR COUNTRY

Rise it will.

The foundation good—it may yet be SAVED.

The FEDERAL EDIFICE.

ELEVEN STARS, in quick succession rise—
ELEVEN COLUMNS strike our wond'ring eyes,
Soon o'er the *whole*, shall swell the beauteous DOME,
COLUMBIA's boast—and FREEDOM's hallow'd home.
Here shall the ARTS in glorious splendour shine !
And AGRICULTURE give her stores divine !
COMMERCE refin'd, dispense us more than gold,
And this new world, teach WISDOM to the old—
RELIGION here shall fix her blest abode,
Array'd in *mildness*, like its parent GOD !
JUSTICE and LAW, shall endless PEACE maintain,
And *the* " SATURNIAN AGE," *return again.*

The Federal Pillars, *an engraving that appeared in* The Massachusetts Centinel *on August 2, 1788. To mark each state's ratification of the Constitution, the newspaper published an illustration showing upright columns inscribed with the state's name. Upon discovering that their products would be treated as foreign goods unless they joined the Union, North Carolina and Rhode Island ratified the Constitution in 1789.*

responsible for promoting the commercial interests of the United States, would serve as one member of the council. The convention did not adopt Morris's recommendation, and the Constitution makes no explicit provision for a secretary of commerce. Nevertheless, the document, which gave birth to the United States and has served as an inspiration and a model for democracies throughout the world, had its origins, in part, in an urgent need to solve practical problems of trade and commerce.

Just as commercial concerns provided the impetus for the convention and for the Constitution itself, they also were instrumental in persuading all 13 states to ratify the Constitution and join the Union. The last two states to do so—North Carolina and Rhode Island—finally decided to endorse the Constitution when they discovered that unless they joined the Union, their products would be treated as foreign goods, thereby subject to duties and other import regulations.

The New Government Seeks to
Improve Commerce

Soon after George Washington took office as the first president of the United States in 1789, the executive branch of the federal government was organized to include the Department of Foreign Affairs (which later became the Department of State); the War Department (which later became the Department of Defense); the Treasury Department; and an attorney general (who later headed the Justice Department). The Treasury Department was responsible for all matters relating to business and commerce.

The nation's first Treasury secretary, 34-year-old Alexander Hamilton, lacked any formal training or practical experience in finance or economics. Nevertheless, he developed an impressive and effective fiscal plan for the new nation. By establishing the dollar as the national monetary unit, Hamilton eliminated the commercial chaos created by the various currencies issued by the states. He persuaded Congress to assume the debts that the states had incurred during the revolutionary war, as well as those of the federal government under the Articles of Confederation. Congress agreed to shoulder responsibility for approximately $75 million in debt, a substantial sum at that time. But, as Hamilton predicted, by creating immediate faith in the new U.S. government, Congress firmly established the new nation as a good credit risk, ensuring that it would be able to borrow money in the future.

Hamilton believed that government initiative was necessary to ensure that the country would develop its own industries and become economically independent from Europe. As Treasury secretary, he pursued many programs to promote the commercial interests of the nation. He recommended the creation of a central bank to serve as the fiscal foundation of the national economy. Congress approved the plan, and the First Bank of the United States opened in 1791. The bank assisted the federal government by acting as a repository for tax collections, dispensed government salaries, controlled the issuance of paper money, and generally assisted in administering the repayment of the national debt. Hamilton was also convinced that the nation would achieve power and prosperity as an industrial, rather than an agricultural, economy. In his Report on Manufactures (December 5, 1791), he encouraged Congress to enact tariffs to protect infant industries. The protective tariffs would provide U.S. businesses in such emerging industries as textiles with a domestic market for their goods until they could develop sufficiently in technology, skill, and size to compete effectively with European manufacturers. Congress, however, did not adopt this proposal.

Alexander Hamilton, the nation's first Treasury secretary (1789–94), believed that the federal government had to encourage industrial development in order for the United States to become economically independent from Europe.

The Nation Expands

In the first half of the 19th century, the United States expanded rapidly. A cotton boom during the second decade of the century brought prosperity and population to the Deep South. Canals and railroads opened the interior of the continent for economic development and migration. Homesteaders spread throughout the Midwest and the Great Lakes region. Settlements also arose in the West when the gold rush began in California in 1849. By 1853, when the United States purchased the southern regions of New Mexico and Arizona from Mexico, the nation extended from the Atlantic to the Pacific Ocean, and its southern and northern borders were established. The nation and its territories encompassed a population of more than 23 million people, an increase from 9.6 million in 1820.

A boat passes through the Erie Canal when it was opened to traffic in 1825. The canal, which links the Great Lakes to the port of New York City, provided a route for manufactured goods to be transported west to the nation's interior and for agricultural products to be shipped to the East Coast.

As the second half of the 19th century unfolded, the responsibilities of the U.S government also grew in areas relating to trade and commerce. In response to the mounting needs of businesses, several new executive agencies were organized. In 1884, Congress established the Bureau of Labor to represent the concerns of American workers. The bureau compiled comprehensive statistics on national employment levels, wage scales, work hours, and industrial accidents, and it prepared reports on such topics as industrial depressions and divorce rates among workers. The Department of Agriculture, created in 1862 to conduct research and provide information that would improve farming, was elevated to cabinet status in 1889. Agriculture thus became the first industry to have its interests recognized through membership in the growing family of federal agencies.

The second half of the century, particularly between the Civil War and the turn of the century, was marked by further commercial expansion. Banking, business, and industry grew by leaps and bounds. The railroad, textile, and steel industries were particularly successful. For example, railroads expanded from 30,000 miles of track in 1860 to 193,000 in 1900. Investment in new industries generated more profits and prosperity. The gross national product (GNP)—the measure of the total value of all goods and services produced in the United States in one year—rose from less than $5 billion in 1850 to $88 billion in 1900.

Nevertheless, there was a dark side to the American economy and its social life. Great inequities arose in the distribution of newly created wealth. Fully 20 percent of the nation's riches were concentrated in the hands of fewer than 4,000 families and individuals. It was a time of palatial homes and vast teeming slums, of untold luxury and demoralizing sweatshops. Many children worked 10-hour days—often in dangerous mines and factories—for meager wages. Periodic recessions and stock market crashes rocked the economy, causing hardship for most and financial ruin for many. For example, the panic of 1893, a stock market crash triggered by the sudden depletion of the nation's gold reserve, caused a depression that gripped the nation for three years. Many small businesses went bankrupt, and high unemployment and labor unrest were rampant.

In response to the serious economic problems caused by stock market crashes and business cycles, the National Association of Manufacturers—an organization of U.S. businesses that joined together to foster trade, business, and financial interests—lobbied strongly for creation of a department of commerce and industry that would help correct some of the more obvious ills

Locomotives of the Union Pacific and Central Pacific railroads meet on May 10, 1869, at Promontory Point, Utah, marking the completion of the first transcontinental railroad. Railroads were a catalyst for the rapid growth of the nation's economy during the second half of the 19th century.

of the economy. Congress, however, chose instead to establish the U.S. Industrial Commission in 1898 to investigate economic and social issues, including the impact of trusts (combinations of business firms that fix prices and inhibit competition) and monopolies on the national welfare.

The Need for a Department of Commerce

By 1900, the total value of manufactured products in the United States exceeded $13 billion. President William McKinley's policy of actively promoting exports resulted in tripling the value of American manufactured goods sold abroad. Total foreign commerce passed the $1 billion mark, and, for the first time, the value of American goods exported surpassed the value of goods imported into the United States.

Government regulation of economic activity had also gained increasing acceptance at the beginning of the 20th century. Presidents William Howard Taft and Theodore Roosevelt enforced new laws against trusts. Reporters known as muckrakers exposed socioeconomic problems, such as the exploitation of workers and the sale of impure food and drugs. Congress responded by enacting laws to prevent such practices. Although many business and government leaders pointed out that all other industrialized countries had established government agencies to assist business and promote foreign trade, Congress still resisted proposals to establish a Department of Commerce.

In his first State of the Union message in 1901, President Theodore Roosevelt called for the creation of a combined Department of Commerce and Labor, which would be empowered to investigate corporate abuses and to safeguard the rights of workers. After considerable debate and compromise, Congress finally approved legislation on February 14, 1903, that created the Department of Commerce and Labor, and President Roosevelt signed the bill the same day.

At its inception, the new department was at once among the largest and most complex organizations in government. It included the following:

- The Bureau of Corporations, which monitored trusts under the Sherman Antitrust Act of 1890, prohibiting the restraint of trade through the use of unfair methods of competition such as price-fixing.
- The Bureau of Immigration, which enforced immigration laws.
- The Bureau of Navigation, which monitored merchant vessels.

- The Lighthouse Board, which maintained lighthouses to facilitate safe navigation.
- The Steamboat Inspection Service, which inspected steamships to ensure the safety of waterborne commerce.
- The Bureau of Statistics, which compiled and published statistics on foreign and domestic commerce.
- The Coast and Geodetic Survey, which determined the size and shape of the states and coastal areas.
- The Bureau of Standards, which ensured the accuracy of measurements.
- The Bureau of the Census, which counted the population.
- The Bureau of Fisheries, which supervised fisheries and the Alaskan seal-fur trade.

The previously independent Labor Department was transferred to the new Department of Commerce and Labor and renamed the Bureau of Labor. It collected information on hours of labor, earnings, and means of promoting the material and social well-being of workers.

The newest cabinet department was responsible for some of the oldest programs administered by the federal government. Congress had authorized the maintenance of lighthouses in 1789. The first census, as required by the Constitution to determine how the seats in the House of Representatives would be divided among the states, was taken in 1790. Thomas Jefferson signed legislation in 1807 that provided for a survey of the coast. And the Treasury Department had collected statistics on foreign commerce since 1820 and in 1836 had organized an Office of Weights and Measures, whose responsibilities for assuring accuracy of measurements was now lodged in the Bureau of Standards.

President Roosevelt nominated George B. Cortelyou as the new department's first secretary. Cortelyou, who had been the president's personal secretary, was sworn into office on February 18, 1903. He served only one year before leaving in 1904 to manage Roosevelt's campaign for reelection. California congressman Victor H. Metcalf, who served as secretary from July 1904 until December 1906, succeeded Cortelyou. Oscar S. Straus, former U.S. ambassador to Turkey, served as the next secretary of commerce and labor until March 1909. Charles Nagel, a former Missouri Supreme Court justice who served as secretary from March 1909 until Congress split the Department of Commerce and Labor in March 1913 into two separate entities,

President Theodore Roosevelt (1901–9) convinced Congress to create the Department of Commerce and Labor in 1903. The new department was placed in charge of a wide variety of programs and agencies, ranging from the Bureau of Immigration to the Bureau of Fisheries.

A Bureau of the Census clerk processes a questionnaire during the 1910 census. The bureau, which had conducted population counts since 1790, became part of the Department of Commerce and Labor in 1903.

presided over a department that quickly assumed critical functions in areas ranging from science and sociology to commerce and statistics.

During its 10 years of existence, the Department of Commerce and Labor was called upon to play an important role in promoting development of markets for the nation's expanding manufacturing sector. The Bureau of Manufactures, which was responsible for finding foreign markets for American products, was added in 1905. By 1912, manufactured goods accounted for 47 percent of exports. That year, the total value of exports exceeded $1 billion for the first time. The Bureau of Foreign and Domestic Commerce, which provided marketing information to U.S. businesses and conducted trade fairs abroad to promote U.S. goods, was also created in 1912. It would become one of the department's most important divisions in dealing with commercial matters.

At the same time, as workers moved in ever-greater numbers from farms to factories, labor leaders began to agitate for a separation of the department's dual commerce and labor functions. The department was founded on the notion that if one government body worked with both industry and labor, it could help bosses and workers resolve their differences. In reality, the Bureau of Labor, which accounted for only one percent of the staff members in the department, had little power in a department headed by businessmen and devoted mostly to commercial interests. Reacting to the pressure from labor unions, President William Howard Taft signed legislation on March 4, 1913, his last day in office, that split the combined department. Congress granted the Department of Labor cabinet status, and the erstwhile Department of Commerce and Labor now became the Department of Commerce. More than a century after the ratification of the Constitution, Congress had at last established an executive department devoted exclusively to the nation's manufacturing and commercial interests.

Chevrolet cars and trucks sit on the assembly line in Flint, Michigan, in 1920. By the end of the 1920s, more than 3 million workers—from road builders and truck drivers to steel and oil workers—earned their livelihood in connection with the growing U.S. automobile fleet.

THREE

Growth and Development

The new Department of Commerce, with the Bureau of Labor removed, now consisted of the Bureaus of Corporations, Foreign and Domestic Commerce, the Census, Navigation, Lighthouses, and Fisheries, as well as the Coast and Geodetic Survey and Steamboat Inspection Service. On March 5, 1913, President Woodrow Wilson appointed William C. Redfield as the first secretary of commerce. Redfield—a New York businessman, former member of Congress, and author of an influential business book, *The New Industrial Day*—was a dynamic administrator who immediately initiated several important programs. First, commercial attachés were assigned to U.S. embassies in countries that were key trading partners. The attachés, who were experienced in business matters and often bilingual, were responsible for identifying commercial opportunities abroad and for assisting American businesses in taking advantage of them. Second, the department sent knowledgeable industry specialists abroad to conduct market studies. These studies provided useful and much-needed information to U.S. firms seeking to enter foreign markets. Convinced that U.S. manufacturers did not adequately apply science to industry, Redfield also actively supported expansion of the Bureau of Standards, which was responsible for working with industry, universities, and other government agencies to accelerate efforts in research and the development and application of technology. Department of Commerce branch offices were opened in eight major cities: New York, Boston, Atlanta, Chicago, New Orleans, St. Louis, San Francisco, and Seattle. The branch offices helped bring the agency's services directly to American businesses.

With the entrance of the United States into World War I in 1917, the commercial attachés, as well as the scientists employed by the Department of Commerce, were enlisted to provide data that would assist the military in developing war-related materials and equipment. Sixty ships operated by the department's Coast and Geodetic Survey and the Bureau of Lighthouses assisted the U.S. Navy. For example, the department's steamships were used

William C. Redfield, the first secretary of commerce (1913–19), expanded the department's efforts to promote trade by assigning commercial attachés to U.S. embassies abroad. The attachés identified commercial opportunities in other countries and helped U.S. businesses capitalize on them.

for minesweeping, and, in one dramatic incident, a Commerce Department vessel participated in disabling the German submarine that in 1915 had sunk the British liner *Lusitania*. The Census Bureau also contributed to the war effort, supplying records to determine the number of males who were eligible for the draft and providing important data on the nation's manufacturing capabilities. The Bureau of Standards developed a lightweight cotton blanket for the military that replaced its heavier wool blanket. The Bureau of Fisheries helped by promoting the increased consumption of seafood. A campaign to recycle waste paper, initiated by the Commerce Department before the war, was accorded special emphasis during the war years.

After the war, Congress cut appropriations for all research by the Commerce Department. Secretary Redfield resigned in October 1919, and President Wilson appointed Joshua W. Alexander as his successor. Alexander, a congressman from Missouri, stepped down 17 months later when Republican president Warren G. Harding took office.

The Hoover Years

In March 1921, President Harding appointed Herbert Hoover as secretary of commerce. Hoover, who was trained as an engineer, had gained the respect of government officials and earned widespread popularity throughout the world for his brilliant service as chairman of the American Relief Administration and the European Relief Council. Those agencies were responsible for providing food and other necessities to the refugees and victims of World War I in Europe. As commerce secretary, Hoover demonstrated great vision and executive ability—traits that would ultimately carry him all the way to the White House, as the 31st president. During a decade of declining government expenditures, Hoover managed to persuade Congress to increase the department's appropriation from $860,000 in 1920 to more than $5 million in 1928. By the end of his tenure, Hoover had expanded the department's staff fivefold.

Hoover rejected the view of his friend and former secretary of commerce and labor Oscar Straus, who observed that the office required only a couple of hours of work a day and "no other qualification than to be able to put the fish to bed at night and turn on the lights around the coast." Instead, Hoover was determined to expand foreign commerce through greater productivity and better business methods. He also wanted to make the Department of Commerce one of the most important and powerful agencies in the federal government. Hoover's mission was made easier because he assumed office at

Herbert Hoover served as secretary of commerce from March 1921 to August 1928. During his tenure, the department grew tremendously, serving U.S. businesses as an indispensible source of information and assistance.

a time when new inventions and entirely new industries, particularly automobile manufacturing, were beginning to transform American life. Government licensing and regulation of business, as well as the adoption of safety rules and other operating requirements, were urgently needed to protect workers and consumers.

Under Hoover, the Department of Commerce began to expand immediately. In 1921, as part of Hoover's program to turn the Census Bureau into an effective statistical agency, the Department of Commerce began a reporting program that involved publishing key economic data, including balance of payments information. Balance of payments refers to the amount of money that flows in and out of a country, including the value of imports and exports, loans and investments, and income from tourism. This program has evolved into the comprehensive system of economic measurements upon which millions of government officials, economists, corporate planners, and investors now rely. The next year, Congress added a building and housing division to the department, which collected and disseminated data on the construction industry. In 1926, the Commerce Department began operation of an aeronautics branch (the forerunner of the Federal Aviation Administration), which was responsible for regulating air commerce and controlling the use of the nation's airspace. The following year the department established a radio division to end confusion over assignment of radio frequencies and to foster the new communications medium. The radio division would later become a basic component of the Federal Communications Commission, an independent regulatory agency that was created in 1934.

As a result of his experiences in Europe as relief administrator and earlier in Asia as an engineer and businessman, Hoover was convinced of the importance of exports to the American economy. Accordingly, he enlarged the department's trade-promotion activities. The Bureau of Foreign and Domestic Commerce grew to a system of 50 offices that spanned the globe. Its employees prepared reports that presented and analyzed information on the tariffs and commercial laws of other countries. The reports also provided credit ratings of foreign businesses. The bureau became an indispensable source of information and advice for U.S. businesses. In the dozen years between 1913 and 1925, America's foreign trade had increased by one-third. By 1927, the Department of Commerce was responding to nearly 2.4 million inquiries from businesses about potential markets. In one especially noteworthy success, the department was able to find an eager market in Japan for California's huge rice surplus.

41

Passengers prepare to board a Pan American Airways airplane in the 1920s. In 1926, Congress created an aeronautics division in the Department of Commerce, which was responsible for regulating commercial airlines. The aeronautics division was the forerunner of the Federal Aviation Administration.

During the 1920s, the growing size and complexity of the industrial workplace and the increasing use of electricity for a wide variety of purposes led to a greater consciousness of the need for national safety codes. The Department of Commerce participated in a major effort to develop safety codes to reduce industrial accidents and to help assure safe installation and use of electrical equipment. By expanding its earlier responsibility for safe ocean travel, the department also helped develop traffic signals as well as rules and standards for safe road and air travel—both modern modes of transportation that were beginning to experience marked growth following World War I.

By the late 1920s, economists documented an important new trend in the American economy: the beginning of a shift in the work force from manufacturing occupations to sales, professional, and personal services. The Department of Commerce also noted another trend in its annual report for 1928: In addition to those directly involved in auto manufacturing, 3 million workers owed their livelihood to America's growing fleet of motor vehicles. These

42

included auto sales agents, service attendants, road builders, commercial truck operators, and taxi and bus drivers. Industries that provided materials for the manufacture of cars—such as those producing iron and steel, rubber, glass, and petroleum products—flourished.

The nation had prospered under the administrations of Republican presidents Harding and Calvin Coolidge. The income of U.S. families and the productivity of businesses increased rapidly. The prices of farm products were rising. It was the age of prosperity, and a sense of economic and social infallibility pervaded the nation as population and wealth continued to expand. Herbert Hoover, riding a crest of popularity as a politician associated with a boom economy, was elected president in 1928.

In 1925, a driver heeds a newly installed traffic signal on a Washington, D.C., street. During the 1920s, the Department of Commerce participated in a number of programs to improve public safety, including the development of uniform traffic signals and rules.

A Victorian parlor in an opulent Washington, D.C., home in the 1920s. The Roaring Twenties was a decade of prosperity and progress in which the nation's population and wealth expanded immensely.

The Great Depression

On October 21, 1929, 10 months after Hoover's inauguration, the most devastating stock market crash in the nation's history occurred. The Great Depression—a steep economic decline that lasted for more than a decade—followed. It created substantially more economic misery and dislocation than had ever before been experienced in the nation's history. By 1932, the national income had declined by more than half its 1929 level—from $87.4 billion to $41.7 billion. Production of goods and services plunged more than 40 percent. Trade with foreign nations reached its lowest point since the Department of Commerce was created in 1913 as American exports fell by 34 percent and imports by 37 percent. From 1929 to 1933, 125,000 businesses failed. In 1933, 14 million Americans (one-quarter of all workers) were unemployed.

Franklin D. Roosevelt was elected president in 1932, at a time when private enterprise and businessmen were viewed by the public with an increasing degree of anger and suspicion. Roosevelt appointed Daniel C. Roper, who had held a number of government posts (most recently commissioner of the Internal Revenue Service), as secretary of commerce. Roper observed that the department was "important under normal times, [but suffered] from the fact that business was in the doghouse." Following a program to cut expenses, Roper closed 21 of the 53 field offices of the Bureau of Foreign and Domestic Commerce. Senator Sam G. Bratton of New Mexico proposed that a joint House and Senate committee be formed to consider abolishing the Department of Commerce and transferring its indispensable divisions to other agencies.

Bratton's proposal was ignored, and the Department of Commerce survived. The Roosevelt administration charged it with the responsibility of assisting various programs of the New Deal—as the economic recovery programs

People wait in line for bread and milk in Grand Rapids, Michigan, in December 1931. During the Great Depression—the long, steep economic decline triggered by the stock market crash of October 21, 1929—many businesses failed and millions of American workers were left unemployed.

A cartoon showing Uncle Sam uniting employees and employers promotes the National Recovery Administration (NRA). The NRA was a major component of President Franklin Roosevelt's New Deal, a program designed to pull the country out of the Great Depression.

introduced by the Roosevelt administration were called. The department was especially involved with the National Recovery Administration (NRA). The NRA was responsible for carrying out the mandate of the National Industrial Recovery Act, which Congress passed to improve the economy by allowing the president to establish and enforce codes of fair competition that regulated minimum prices, wages, plant construction, and other business factors. The codes would be approved by industrial organizations or trade associations before the president adopted them. The NRA helped the economy recover but proved unpopular with consumers because high prices were established; with small-business owners because big business was given a dominant voice in setting the codes; and with conservatives because they felt that the legislation created an unreasonable intrusion of the government into business. Critics of the legislation carried their opposition all the way to the U.S. Supreme Court, which declared the National Industrial Recovery Act unconstitutional in *Schecter Poultry Corp. v. U.S.* (1935).

Still out of favor with New Dealers and the Roosevelt administration, the Department of Commerce was stripped of several important components and functions. The Bureau of Air Commerce was transferred to the Civil Aeronautics Authority in 1938. The next year, the Bureau of Lighthouses was assigned to the U.S. Coast Guard, a part of the Treasury Department; the Bureau of Fisheries was transferred to the Department of the Interior; and the Foreign Commerce Service was moved to the Department of State.

But with the first rumblings of war in Europe, the fortunes of the Department of Commerce began to improve. Business recovery was under way, and the services of the department would soon be needed for America's imminent participation in the war. In 1940, the U.S. Weather Service, which

A weather observation airplane, equipped with measurement instruments and recorders on its wings, returns from a mission in the 1940s. The National Weather Service, which was established in 1891, was transferred from the Department of Agriculture to the Department of Commerce in 1940.

had been part of the Department of Agriculture, and the Civil Aeronautics Administration (CAA) became agencies within the department. Following the Japanese attack on Pearl Harbor on December 7, 1941, the United States declared war on Japan and entered World War II. The Commerce Department made a number of essential contributions to the war effort. It worked with industry on ways to increase war-plant production. For example, the Bureau of Standards developed uniform standards to ensure the interchangeability of parts for guns, tanks, and aircraft. Bureau scientists also designed the proximity fuze (an electronic device that uses radio waves to detonate a bomb when it comes close to its target) and an early version of the guided missile. The CAA expanded its pilot training programs to accommodate flight cadets of the army and navy. The department provided the military service with maps, meteorological information, and other data. And the Department of Commerce supervised the National Inventors Council, which helped screen inventions, ideas, and other suggestions to identify those with potential military value.

Supporting the Postwar Economy

Following the collapse of Nazi Germany in 1945, the Department of Commerce became the repository for more than 3.5 billion pages of captured German documents, many of them dealing with scientific and technical subjects. It was also made custodian of 300,000 pounds of German equipment and product samples. The department's National Technical Information Service (NTIS), which now disseminates scientific and technical information to businesses, is an outgrowth of the Office of Declassification and Technical Services, the program that made the captured German data available to American industry.

As a means by which to help foreign countries rebuild their war-torn economies, Commerce's Office of International Trade began to encourage the importation of goods to America from abroad. For the same reason, Americans were encouraged to engage in foreign tourism. However, in 1949, the department imposed controls on the export of certain goods that were believed to have important military or strategic value. This program—which still remains part of the foreign policy of the United States—was adopted to ensure that new technologies would not be made available to the Soviet Union and other potential adversaries. The department continued to play an important role in protecting the nation's defense technology during the cold war—the period from the late 1940s to the mid-1980s that was marked by political, economic, and social tension between the United States and its Western European allies and the Soviet Union and its Eastern European allies.

Hundreds of cars jam the freeways in Los Angeles. The Department of Commerce began the planning and construction of the nation's interstate highway system in the 1950s. The newly created Department of Transportation assumed responsibility for interstate highways in 1967.

The Department of Commerce also assumed a key role in the transition of the American economy from war to peace. By the early 1950s, the department became the federal government's principal transportation agency when the Bureau of Public Roads (1949) and the Maritime Administration (1950) were transferred to it. In 1949, the department also established the Office of Transportation, which was responsible for coordinating transportation information and law. The nation's great interstate highway system was begun under the department's guidance in the 1950s; however, Congress passed the Interstate Highway Act in 1967, transferring this responsibility to the newly created Department of Transportation.

During the Korean War (1950–53), the Department of Commerce coordinated and encouraged defense production, primarily by allocating scarce materials for defense needs. At the same time, the Bureau of Standards worked with manufacturers to standardize sizes of containers for frozen fruits and vegetables and to develop a new system of sizes for women's clothing.

In 1956, Commerce Department experts assisted in renegotiating the General Agreement on Tariffs and Trade (GATT), the international accord between countries that participate in more than 80 percent of world trade. GATT prescribes a code of conduct for governments in international trade and provides a forum for the settlement of trade disputes between nations that have signed the agreement. After many rounds of negotiation, GATT has substantially reduced tariffs and other trade barriers. Recent GATT negotiations have focused on the economic problems of developing countries. As a result, developing countries, such as Jamaica and India, may impose higher tariffs on imported goods, an action that protects their emerging industries from the competition of foreign-made products.

In 1961, the department reported that world trade had reached a record high. At the same time, U.S. exports peaked at $19.9 billion, and imports declined to $13.9 billion. Luther H. Hodges, President John F. Kennedy's secretary of commerce, carried out a broad reorganization of the Bureau of Foreign Commerce to focus on promoting even more exports. The first of five American overseas trade centers was opened in London in 1961. The center successfully promoted $1 billion in sales of American products in its first week of operation. Commerce experts also conducted trade clinics for businessmen throughout the nation, and the president's "E" award was established to recognize American manufacturers that were highly successful in promoting exports.

Two new programs, which would later become permanent fixtures of the department, were also undertaken by Commerce in 1961. The department initiated a pilot project to stimulate development in economically depressed areas of the country, such as rural Appalachia and inner-city slums. This program became the Economic Development Administration, which was formally established in 1965. The U.S. Travel Service, which became the U.S. Travel and Tourism Administration in 1981, was created to promote the United States as a destination for foreign tourists. By 1969, more than 1.5 million foreigners visited the United States, an increase of more than 230 percent from 1961. In the early 1960s, the department also supervised U.S. participation in 2 world fairs—the Century 21 Exposition in Seattle and the New York World's Fair.

During the Vietnam War (1955–75), the Department of Commerce, though less involved in this war than in other conflicts in the 20th century, contributed to the war effort by supplying more than 100 ships from the Maritime Administration's National Defense Reserve Fleet. The ships were used to transport supplies to American forces in Southeast Asia.

Luther H. Hodges, secretary of commerce from 1961 to 1965, reorganized the department to improve its efforts to promote exports. He also directed the creation of pilot programs to bolster the U.S. tourism industry and to stimulate development in economically depressed areas of the country.

51

Tractors carry farmers, including one wearing a Jimmy Carter mask, during a 1980 march protesting the president's order that prohibited the export of grain to the Soviet Union. The Soviet invasion of Afghanistan in 1979 prompted Carter to impose trade restrictions, including a grain embargo, against the Soviet Union.

When President Richard M. Nixon appointed banker Maurice Stans as secretary of commerce in 1969, the department was composed of 16 divisions with more than 25,000 employees. Surprisingly, less than four percent of the department's resources were used to stimulate and regulate international trade. Under Stans, the department reorganized and launched several new programs. The National Oceanic and Atmospheric Administration (NOAA), a scientific agency responsible for weather forecasting, ocean charting, oceanographic research, and other related activities, was created in 1970. NOAA consolidated the duties of various Commerce Department programs and five other agencies in one body. In 1971, Nixon issued an executive order that established the Office of Minority Business Enterprise, a program to help minority-owned firms become established and succeed in business. This office would be renamed the Minority Business Development Agency (MBDA) in 1979.

For the first time since statistics had been kept, the United States recorded a negative balance of trade in 1971—a troublesome trend that has continued to the present day. In an effort to alleviate this problem and as a reflection of a relaxation of the cold war, the department promoted trade with the Soviet Union, and trade barriers were relaxed. The department also sought to stimulate trade with the People's Republic of China and Eastern Europe. By the end of the decade, however, President Jimmy Carter's administration imposed trade sanctions—such as a grain embargo—on the Soviet Union in response to the Soviet invasion of Afghanistan.

In 1974, Congress created the National Fire Prevention and Control Administration, a research program that supported state and local fire authorities, and placed it within the Department of Commerce. It later became a part of the Federal Emergency Management Administration, an independent agency.

In the 1980s, under the leadership of Secretary of Commerce Malcolm Baldridge, the department became a major force in formulating national economic policy. It took a leading role in supporting passage of the Export Trading Company Act of 1982, which was designed to encourage entry by small- and medium-sized firms into the export business. Baldridge also arranged trade conferences with the leaders of other nations. For example, in a six-day period in June 1985, Baldridge met with General Secretary Mikhail Gorbachev of the Soviet Union, Premier Zhao Ziyang of the People's Republic of China, and Prime Minister Rajiv Gandhi of India. That same year, President Ronald Reagan assigned the commerce secretary to chair a cabinet-level Trade Strike Force to investigate unfair trading practices and to recommend corrective measures.

In 1987, Congress created the Bureau of Export Administration (BXA), giving it responsibility for national export-control policies that helped ensure national security. The new agency improved the enforcement of export laws.

By the end of the 1980s, the Department of Commerce retained only four of the agencies that were originally assigned to it: the Coast and Geodetic Survey, renamed the National Ocean Service; the Bureau of Fisheries,

Under Secretary Malcolm Baldridge (1981–87), the Department of Commerce became a major force in formulating national economic policy. For example, the department took a leading role in conducting trade conferences with the leaders of other nations.

renamed the National Marine Fisheries Service; the National Bureau of Standards, renamed the National Institute of Standards and Technology (NIST); and the Bureau of the Census. As the department entered the 1990s, it was responsible for a wide variety of programs. Although some of them are as old as the Constitution, others are as new as the space age. All of the programs are designed to assist the business community and the nation in meeting the economic and technological challenges that face the country today and those that will be encountered in the 21st century.

An employee of the National Institute of Standards and Technology (NIST) searches for information in NIST's microfilm library. The Department of Commerce provides a wide range of economic and technical information to U.S. businesses.

FOUR

Inside the Department

The Department of Commerce is composed of many distinct subunits that carry out its mission to encourage technological advancement and economic growth and to promote the nation's international trade. The secretary of commerce—whose offices are located in the imposing Herbert Clark Hoover Building in downtown Washington, D.C.—guides the overall policy of the department. The president of the United States, with the advice and consent of the Senate, appoints the secretary of commerce, his or her senior staff, and all of the department's assistant and under secretaries. This arrangement allows the Senate to reject presidential appointees who it feels are unqualified or otherwise unacceptable, although the Senate rarely invokes this power. Presidential appointees to the Commerce Department, as is generally the case for all departments and agencies in the executive branch, may remain in office as long as the president who appointed them wishes. With a change in administrations, appointees customarily resign, making way for the new president's personnel choices. The vast majority of Commerce Department employees, however, are members of the career civil service. They typically obtain their positions in competition with other job applicants and may remain with the department through successive presidential terms and administrations.

The Office of the Secretary

The secretary of commerce, a member of the president's cabinet, directs the execution of all the functions and authorities assigned to the Department of Commerce. The secretary also advises the president on all federal policies and programs that affect the industrial and commercial sectors of the national economy. A deputy secretary assists the secretary, performing special duties and heading the department in the secretary's absence.

The general counsel is the department's chief legal adviser and provides the secretary and the heads of departmental divisions with legal advice on all matters involving the programs of the department (except for issues relating to the issuance of patents and the registration of trademarks). The general counsel heads the Office of General Counsel (OGC), which is responsible for identifying and resolving legal issues affecting American productivity, competitiveness, and technology. The OGC advises Commerce officials on a wide range of issues involving the use of funds, labor relations, litigation, complex financial matters, and general management problems. The OGC also prepares or reviews all proposed rules, legislation, and official communications that the department sends to Congress.

The Office of Congressional and Intergovernmental Affairs advises the secretary of commerce on matters relating to Congress and state and local governments. The Office of Congressional Affairs (OCA) provides information and advice to Commerce Department officials on legislation affecting their programs. It shares responsibility with the OGC for handling the department's legislative programs. The OCA also coordinates all department activities involving Congress. For example, in 1988 the OCA assisted with the U.S.-Canada Free Trade Agreement (FTA), which went into effect January 1, 1989. Under the FTA, tariffs between the United States and Canada would be phased out over the next 10 years. The FTA assures the free movement of goods, services, and investments between the two countries. For example, the FTA guarantees U.S. purchasers a right to buy Canadian oil and gas at the same price and with the same access as Canadian purchasers. Intergovernmental Affairs (IGA) coordinates the Department of Commerce's activities with state and local officials. For example, the IGA initiated and helped coordinate meetings of regional, state, and local elected officials to discuss problems posed by the Bureau of the Census's 1990 population count.

Two offices keep the secretary of commerce informed of administrative issues and problems. The assistant secretary for administration is the principal adviser to the secretary and the deputy secretary on such administrative

A pumper fills a U.S. tanker with Canadian oil in Windsor, Ontario. The Department of Commerce's Office of Congressional Affairs provided recommendations for the negotiations of the U.S.-Canada Free Trade Agreement. Under the pact, which was signed in 1989, trade barriers between the two countries will be phased out to encourage the free movement of goods, services, and investment.

matters as management, budget, program evaluation, personnel, and accounting. In addition, the inspector general searches for problems in the administration of the department and recommends solutions to those problems. To prevent the waste and misuse of government funds, the Office of Inspector General conducts audits and investigations of departmental programs.

The other staff offices of the secretary of commerce include the Office of Public Affairs, which is responsible for the department's overall public information and communications program, and the Office of Consumer Affairs, which represents consumer interests to the business community and assists business in improving consumer relations. The Office of Business Liaison helps promote a cooperative relationship between the Commerce Department and the business community. It keeps businesses informed about departmental activities and resources and ensures that the secretary and other department officials are always aware of the concerns and interests of U.S. business.

Program Areas

Ten major program areas carry out a wide range of activities to fulfill the Department of Commerce's broad mission to foster, promote, and develop foreign and domestic commerce and the nation's manufacturing industries. The department's areas of interest may be divided into four general categories: science and technology, economic affairs, economic development, and trade. The categories, with the administrations, bureaus, and offices that execute the department's functions, are as follows:

- *Science and technology:* the National Oceanic and Atmospheric Administration, the National Institute of Standards and Technology, the National Telecommunications and Information Administration, and the Patent and Trademark Office.

- *Economic affairs:* the Office of Economic Affairs (which includes the Bureau of Economic Analysis and the Bureau of the Census).

- *Economic development:* the Economic Development Administration and the Minority Business Development Agency.

- *Trade:* the International Trade Administration, the Bureau of Export Administration, and the U.S. Travel and Tourism Administration.

The following material provides a closer look at the 10 functional programs of the Department of Commerce and the work of their constituent organizations, all of which contribute to the nation's economic well-being and the enrichment of the lives of every citizen.

The National Oceanic and Atmospheric Administration

The National Oceanic and Atmospheric Administration (NOAA) gathers data, conducts research, and makes predictions about the environment. NOAA's products and services touch the lives of all Americans: It warns of dangerous weather, charts the seas and skies, and oversees the use and protection of ocean resources. NOAA helps to shape the nation's future by assisting the National Science Foundation and the National Aeronautics and Space Administration (NASA) in the study of the ocean, atmosphere, space, and sun. NOAA also carries out programs designed to improve the nation's safety, welfare, security, and commerce through a better understanding and rational use of the natural environment.

With approximately 13,000 employees, NOAA is the largest agency in the Commerce Department. NOAA accomplishes its work through five major divisions: the National Weather Service; the National Ocean Service; the National Marine Fisheries Service; the National Environmental Satellite Data and Information Service; and the Office of Oceanic and Atmospheric Research.

The National Weather Service is perhaps the organizational element of the Commerce Department that is most familiar to the greatest number of Americans. Although many people, including Benjamin Franklin and Thomas Jefferson, kept weather diaries, the first government collection of weather reports did not begin until 1812, when the surgeon general of the army initiated a program to determine the effects of weather on health. In 1870, Congress created a weather service under the secretary of war. The first daily weather maps appeared in January 1871, and weather predictions began to be published regularly the next month.

The civilian weather service was established in July 1891, when Congress transferred the General Weather Bureau from the army to the Department of

A National Weather Service (NWS) meteorologist uses a satellite photograph to prepare a weather forecast. The NWS initiated a modernization program in 1989 that will provide the public with more timely and accurate weather forecasts and warnings.

Commercial fishing vessels return to port to unload their catches. The National Marine Fisheries Service assists commercial fishing businesses by regulating catches and preventing overfishing.

Agriculture and renamed it the U.S. Weather Bureau. Then, in 1940, the Weather Bureau was moved to the Department of Commerce and began to provide five-day forecasts. During the 1950s, the Weather Bureau established a severe-storm forecast center and began the National Hurricane Research Project, which investigated the nature and causes of hurricanes and ways to improve forecasting of severe storms. In 1960, NASA launched the first weather satellite, and in 1961 the Weather Bureau, in cooperation with the Defense Department and NASA, began the development and operation of a global weather-satellite observation system. In 1970, the Weather Bureau was renamed the National Weather Service (NWS).

Every day, millions of people rely on weather data and predictions from the Weather Service. For example, students decide what to wear to school and farmers plan their crops based on weather predictions. And business commuters—perhaps unknowingly—entrust their safety to the accuracy of data supplied by the Weather Service to pilots and air traffic controllers. The

Weather Service also issues warnings to the public when such destructive weather phenomena as floods, hurricanes, and tornadoes threaten lives and property.

After more than a decade of planning, the Weather Service began a $1 billion modernization program in 1989. The renovations included a new radar system, called Nexrad, that detects impending tornadoes and measures the severity of approaching storms; improved satellites; high-speed computers; and 1,000 automated observation units located throughout the country that continuously collect information on temperature, precipitation, wind, and barometric pressure. Weather Service forecasters, equipped with advanced tools for forecasting severe weather systems, are now able to provide more timely and accurate weather forecasts and warnings.

Another division of NOAA, the National Ocean Service was the nation's first scientific agency. Legislation providing for a survey of the coast was approved by Thomas Jefferson in 1807, and work to survey the coast began in 1816. The National Ocean Service produces charts used for air and marine navigation and conducts geodetic surveys to determine land boundaries, an activity that is indispensable to accurate mapping. The service's aircraft and research vessels provide valuable information used to monitor ocean-water quality and to protect marine life. It also operates marine wildlife sanctuaries at certain estuaries—areas where the salt water of the oceans meet the fresh water of rivers—to protect those regions in which most marine life begins.

Because fish was an important source of food, President Ulysses S. Grant signed a bill in 1871 that underscored the nation's interest in fisheries conservation and created the Office of Commissioner of Fish and Fisheries. The agency was later renamed the Bureau of Fisheries when it joined the newly created Department of Commerce and Labor in 1903. The bureau was transferred to the Department of the Interior in 1939 but returned to the Department of Commerce (renamed the National Marine Fisheries Service) in 1970, when NOAA was created. The service assists the commercial fishing industry by regulating catches and preventing overfishing. It is also responsible for protecting marine animals, such as porpoises, whales, and sea turtles.

The National Marine Fisheries Service is now responsible for managing the Magnuson Act, major fisheries legislation that Congress passed in 1976. The act established an exclusive U.S. fishery conservation zone between 3 and 200 miles off the U.S. coast and charged the Commerce Department with management of commercial and recreational fish stocks within that zone. The Magnuson Act has resulted in an increase of the U.S. share of fish caught in the fishery conservation zone, which was formerly dominated by foreign fleets. In 1987, the foreign catch in the 200-mile zone was 328 million pounds, only one-quarter the amount caught the preceding year.

The National Environmental Satellite Data and Information Service operates satellite systems that provide data to assist in accurate weather forecasting and in predicting floods and crop conditions. Climate- and weather-data centers, operated by the service, influence building design, food supplies, and even human health.

An employee of the National Environmental Satellite Data and Information Service prepares to receive a transmission from a weather satellite. The service operates satellite systems that provide environmental information used in weather forecasting and predicting crop conditions.

NOAA's Office of Oceanic and Atmospheric Research conducts basic scientific research vital to our understanding of the environment, including oceanographic and atmospheric research, as well as study of the relationship between the earth and our nearest star, the sun. For example, NOAA scientists continue their studies to determine the cause of a hole in the ozone layer (an environmentally important element of the earth's upper atmosphere) that has developed above Antarctica. The research efforts of NOAA scientists are augmented by university-based scientists who receive funding from the department through the National Sea Grant Program.

The National Institute of Standards and Technology
The National Institute of Standards and Technology (NIST) is the nation's science and engineering laboratory for measurement technology and standards research. Standards are references established to measure quantity, weight, or quality. Accurate measurements are made by comparing the measured quantity against known standard units, such as seconds (time), degrees (temperature), and inches (length).

In 1900, the United States was the only great commercial nation without a national standards laboratory. The next year, Congress created the Bureau of Standards, which was charged with the custody, comparison, and, where necessary, development of standards. The bureau, originally part of the Treasury Department, was also responsible for the testing and calibration (setting) of standard measuring apparatuses, the solutions of problems that arise in connection with standards, and the determination of physical constants and the properties of materials.

Transferred to the Department of Commerce and Labor in 1903, the bureau's earliest efforts included acquiring instruments that were necessary for its research; establishing standards for electricity, a new and important factor in the productivity of American industry; introducing scientific methods to manufacturers; and protecting consumers through the testing of scales, weights, and liquid and dry measures. The bureau was renamed the National Institute of Standards and Technology in 1988.

NIST research has been in the forefront of advances in electricity, aviation, automotive engineering, and materials science—from producing the first alternating current radio set in 1922 to developing an automated laser tracking system in 1988 that simplifies accurate measurement of large objects, such as airplanes and fuel tanks. It has developed better, more accurate standards for length and entirely new standards for measuring light, temperature, and time.

65

In 1989, a physicist conducts an experiment to test a mercury ion clock at a NIST laboratory. NIST researchers invented the world's first atomic clock in 1949 and continue to search for a more accurate standard of timekeeping.

NIST operates several laboratories that help conduct its many research projects. The National Engineering Laboratory is responsible for engineering research, including development of standards for computer-aided design and manufacturing, fire prevention and control, and building construction. The National Measurement Laboratory develops and maintains physical and chemical standards, measurement methods, and related services for use by government, industry, and universities. The Institute for Materials Science and Engineering studies the structure, chemical reactions, and physical properties of materials. Its research provides the basis for advanced materials technology for use by industry. Finally, the National Computer Systems Laboratory conducts research in computer science and automatic data processing and develops policies and standards for computers and related telecommunications systems.

NIST conducts many research projects that affect industry and touch the lives of consumers. For example, in 1988, NIST concluded, after a study conducted at the request of Congress, that an encoding system proposed by CBS Records to prevent prerecorded music from being copied by new digital audiotape (DAT) was inadequate. The system sometimes did not prevent the recording of some material, and some listeners could discern a difference between musical selections that had been coded to prevent recording and those that had not. NIST also found that the copy prevention system could be bypassed easily.

NIST has also developed a standard reference material to help ensure that drug-testing laboratories are producing reliable results when checking urine

Two researchers review manufacturing data in the control room at NIST's Automated Manufacturing Research Facility. The facility is used by NIST for research and technical work related to computer-automated manufacturing.

samples for evidence of marijuana abuse. The bottled material contains a specific concentration of the substance that appears in urine after marijuana use, and it helps laboratories determine whether their analysis equipment is working properly and whether their methods of analyzing urine specimens are providing accurate results.

NIST is a valuable behind-the-scenes partner of industry, providing the standards and measurement techniques that foster technological advance, domestic and international commerce, and, ultimately, economic progress. The research and development conducted by the NIST serves as a technical basis for increasing productivity and innovation, thereby enhancing the competitiveness of American products in world markets. Through its outreach programs, NIST helps U.S. industry adopt and exploit the most efficient technologies that will equip them to meet the demands of global competition.

The National Telecommunications and Information Administration

The National Telecommunications and Information Administration (NTIA) was created in 1978 in response to the explosive growth in communications technology. The NTIA is responsible for developing U.S. policy on the advancement and use of new communications technologies, and it conducts research in radio and other communications systems. The NTIA's goals are to enhance the growth of telecommunications and related industries, provide policy guidance for use of the airways by the federal government, and award grants to public broadcasting organizations to improve their facilities. The NTIA is organized into four departments:

- The Office of International Affairs, which monitors international telecommunications, information, and trade.

- The Office of Policy Analysis and Development, which promotes competition, innovation, and deregulation within the telecommunications and mass media industries.

- The Office of Spectrum Management, which authorizes radio frequency assignments to the agencies of the federal government.

- The Institute for Telecommunications Sciences, which develops domestic and international communications standards and reports on technical advancements.

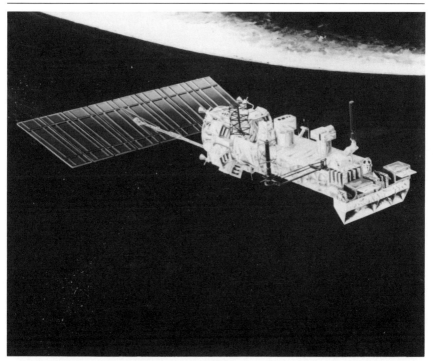

A U.S. satellite relays distress calls from ships and aircraft equipped with emergency beacons. The National Telecommunications and Information Administration develops the Department of Commerce's policy on the use of new communications technology, including satellite communications systems.

The NTIA also administers the Public Telecommunications Facilities Program (PTFP), which makes matching fund grants to assist public television and radio stations in improving their equipment. In 1988, the NTIA awarded 124 PTFP grants to public broadcasting stations in 44 states.

Patent and Trademark Office

The Patent and Trademark Office (PTO) is one of the oldest and most unusual agencies in the federal government. The framers of the Constitution recognized that the nation's economy would have greater potential if they granted a limited patent to protect the interests of inventors. Article I, Section 8, of the Constitution states: "Congress shall have the power . . . to promote the progress of science and useful arts by securing for limited times to . . .

69

inventors the exclusive right to . . . their discoveries." On April 10, 1790, President George Washington signed a bill that established the foundations of the modern American patent system to encourage the exercise of skill and genius. A patent for an invention is a grant of a property right by the government to the inventor for a term of 17 years from the date that the patent is granted. The patent grant confers, in the words of the statute, "the right to exclude others from making, using, or selling" the invention. The statute also defines an invention or discovery that would warrant a patent as "any useful art, manufacture, engine, machine or device, or any improvement thereon not before known or used." The 1790 statute established the Patent Board and made it responsible for administering patent law and examining inventions. The Patent Board—consisting of the secretary of state, the secretary of war, and the attorney general—proved unworkable because its members were involved in more important matters. In 1802, a separate, full-time superintendent of patents, who worked in the State Department, was placed in charge of patents. Congress revised the patent laws in 1836 and placed a new official, the commissioner of patents and trademarks, in charge of administering patent laws. The patent office remained in the State Department until 1849, when it was transferred to the Department of the Interior.

Between 1790 and 1870, nearly 130,000 patents were issued. The years between 1870 and 1900 are considered perhaps the greatest period of invention in U.S. history. The telephone, trolley car, electric light, cash register, and steam turbine were patented during this period. At the turn of the century, U.S. patent holders included Thomas Edison (light bulb and phonograph), Alexander Graham Bell (telephone), Nikola Tesla (electric motor), Guglielmo Marconi (wireless telegraphy), Rudolf Diesel (an internal combustion engine), and Henry Ford (improved carburetors and motor carriages). The patent office was transferred to the Department of Commerce in 1925, and in 1975 its name was officially changed to the Patent and Trademark Office (PTO).

In granting patents for inventions, the PTO administers the patent laws and performs other duties relating to patents. It examines applications for patents to determine if the applicants are legally entitled to them and grants the patents when appropriate. The PTO publishes the specifications of issued patents and produces various publications concerning them. It also records assignments of patents, maintains a search room for the use of the public to examine issued patents and records, and supplies copies of records and other papers relating to patents. The PTO has no jurisdiction over questions of infringement and

Thomas Alva Edison (1847–1931), inventor of the electric light bulb and the phonograph, poses in his laboratory in Menlo Park, New Jersey. The Patent and Trademark Office (PTO) grants patents to inventors such as Edison for their new and useful discoveries. Under federal law, patentees may exclude others from making, using, or selling their invention for a period of 17 years.

enforcement of patents. Patentees must bring suit on their own behalf to seek relief from alleged infringements.

The PTO has about 3,100 employees, of whom about half are examiners and others with technical and legal training. Patent applications are now received at the rate of over 130,000 per year. In 1988 alone, approximately 83,000 patents were issued, allowing inventors to enjoy exclusive rights to their creative efforts. The work of examining applications for patents is divided among a number of examining groups, each one having jurisdiction over certain designated fields of technology. The examiners review applications for patents and determine whether they can be granted. If an examiner rejects an application, the applicant may appeal the decision to the PTO's Board of Patent Appeals.

The PTO performs similar functions with respect to the registration of trademarks. A trademark refers to any word, name, symbol, or device that is used in commerce to indicate the source or origin of the goods and to

Dr. Philip Leder, professor of genetics at Harvard Medical School, shows a photo of a genetically altered mouse. The PTO granted Harvard University a patent on the mouse in 1988, the first time a patent was issued for an animal. The PTO grants approximately 80,000 patents each year.

Borden, Inc.'s Elsie the Cow (left) and the Campbell Soup Company's Kids (only one shown here) are two trademarks. A trademark is any word, name, or symbol used in commerce to indicate the source of goods and to distinguish them from the goods of other producers. (The Campbell Kids are a trademark of Campbell Soup Company.)

distinguish them from the goods of others. Trade names such as Xerox, Nike, and Oreo and product images such as the Pillsbury Doughboy and Kellogg's Tony the Tiger are trademarks. The PTO provides trademark protection to businesses for their corporate or product marks and identifications. Trademark rights may be used to prevent others from using a confusingly similar mark but not to prevent them from making the same goods or from selling them under a nonconfusing mark. More than 58,000 trademarks were registered or renewed in 1988, allowing manufacturers and merchants to identify their goods or services and to distinguish them from those manufactured or sold by others. The trademark system protects manufacturers, vendors, and consumers, serving to prevent unfair competition and consumer deception.

Office of Economic Affairs

Created in 1961 by President John F. Kennedy to coordinate the formulation of U.S. economic policy, the Office of Economic Affairs analyzes economic trends, develops economic policy options, and oversees the collection and dissemination of a major share of demographic statistics gathered by the U.S. government. Its major components, the Bureau of Economic Analysis and the Bureau of the Census, provide economic data, analyses, and forecasts collected by government agencies and private firms. The Office of Economic Affairs also includes the Office of Productivity, Technology, and Innovation, which seeks to advance the productivity, technological innovation, and competitiveness of U.S. businesses, and the National Technical Information Service, which is a clearinghouse for government-sponsored research.

The Bureau of Economic Analysis (BEA), originally named the Bureau of Business Economics, measures U.S. economic activity and provides useful analyses of the economy. Its reports play an important role in the formulation of government economic policy and of the fiscal plans of businesses. To present a clear picture of the U.S. economy, the BEA focuses its efforts on such key issues as economic growth, inflation, regional development, and the nation's role in the world economy. The most widely used statistic produced by the BEA is the gross national product (GNP)—a comprehensive measure of economic activity. The GNP represents the sum total of all goods and services produced in the United States in one year. The BEA produces estimates of total and per capita personal income, which are used by the federal government to distribute funds to the states and municipalities and by businesses in marketing and plant-location studies. The BEA also furnishes regional economic accounts—which provide information on economic activity by region, state, county, and metropolitan area—and international economic accounts, which analyze transactions between the United States and foreign countries, as well as the international investment position of the United States. The BEA provides information needed in formulating U.S. policies on domestic investment and in examining the effect of such investment on production, employment, and trade.

The BEA also tracks business cycles, conducts surveys of capital spending by U.S. companies, and forecasts changes in economic activity. To provide U.S. businesses with the latest economic information and analyses, the BEA produces two monthly publications—*Survey of Current Business* (which was initiated by Commerce secretary Herbert Hoover in 1921) and *Business Conditions Digest*.

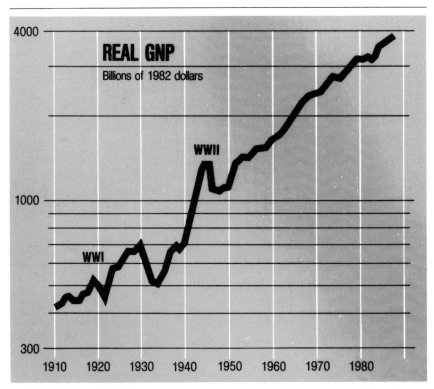

A chart shows the U.S. gross national product (GNP) since 1910. The GNP, which is the sum total of all goods and services produced in the United States in one year, is one of the many useful economic statistics produced by the Bureau of Economic Analysis.

As the U.S. government's principal fact-finding agency, the Bureau of the Census collects, processes, analyzes, and disseminates data on population, housing, manufacturing, transportation, minerals, agriculture, construction, service industries, governments, foreign trade, and other countries. Although best known for its 10-year population counts, the bureau also conducts economic censuses every 5 years. Economic censuses are statistical surveys in areas such as retail trade, wholesale trade, service industries, transportation, manufacturing, mineral industries, and agriculture. The Census Bureau also performs surveys and special studies for other government agencies on topics such as employment, health, housing, child care, crime, and consumer expenditures.

A census enumerator visits a house that did not respond to the 1990 census questionnaire. The Bureau of the Census, the world's largest and most advanced governmental statistical agency, conducts population counts every 10 years and economic censuses every 5 years.

The bureau is the world's largest and most advanced government statistical agency. It collects information by asking questions of households, businesses, and governments. It combines the answers into approximately 2,000 reports a year that cover a wide variety of topics and geographic areas. The statistics that the bureau gathers and interprets are widely used by businesses to identify consumer trends and to develop marketing programs. For example, a U.S. computer-game company used information from one of the bureau's international surveys to determine the potential market for their products among young men who owned TV sets in several Latin American countries. Municipal transportation planners in San Francisco used census information to select bus routes and subway stops and to determine which highways needed widening.

The bureau collects information on many subjects, including:

- *People:* age, race, gender, location, income, education, marital status, occupation, and ancestry and ethnic origins.
- *Businesses:* number of employees, total payroll and income, and products manufactured or sold.
- *Housing and construction:* number of houses and apartments, owners and renters, property value or rent paid, and fuels used.
- *Farms:* number, acreage, livestock, and crop sales.
- *Governments:* revenues and expenditures, taxes, and employment.
- *Other nations:* population, and birth- and death rates.
- *Foreign trade:* exports and imports, origin and destination, and goods shipped.

The decennial (10-year) census of the population, which the Constitution requires and was first conducted in 1790, is used to determine the number of seats to which each state is entitled in the U.S. House of Representatives. State and local governments also use this census data to delineate their own election districts. The population census asks questions about such topics as age and gender, color or race, marital status, citizenship, housing, education, and income and employment status.

The sole purpose of censuses is to secure general statistical information. Federal law requires all U.S. residents and businesses to answer census questions to the best of their knowledge. The answers are strictly confidential: Only Census Bureau employees can look at the forms. No data are published that would reveal the identity or activities of any specific individual, and questionnaires cannot be used for taxation, regulation, or investigation.

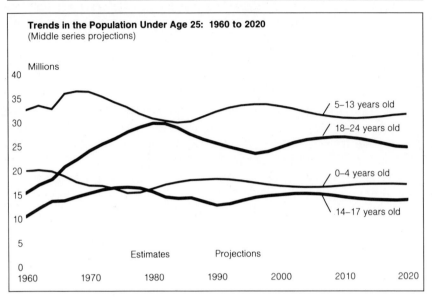

Trends in the Population Under Age 25: 1960 to 2020
(Middle series projections)

Millions

5–13 years old

18–24 years old

0–4 years old

14–17 years old

Estimates   Projections

This Bureau of the Census graph shows the trends in the population under age 25 since 1960 and the projected trends to 2020. The bureau provides information to the public through its many reports and reference materials, including publications such as Population Profile of the United States, World Population Profile, *and* Guide to Foreign Trade Statistics.

Another division of the Office of Economic Affairs, the Office of Productivity, Technology, and Innovation (OPTI), seeks to advance productivity, technological innovation, and competitiveness of U.S. businesses. Its major programs are aimed at fostering partnerships between businesses and the government, stimulating investment in marketing innovations, and promoting private-sector use of inventions generated by the federal government's research and development efforts, which amount to $60 billion annually. The OPTI assists small business groups and state governments in incorporating technology and innovation in economic-development plans and programs. The OPTI's Office of Metric Programs provides assistance, information, and coordination of the national transition to the metric system, calling attention to the important effect that products made with metric dimensions have on the exportability and competitiveness of U.S. products.

The National Technical Information Service (NTIS) had its beginnings in the programs that were created to handle the release of thousands of German technical reports to American industry following World War II. The NTIS is now the government's clearinghouse for scientific, technical, and engineering information that is produced by government-sponsored research. Its collection of research papers and reports exceeds 1.8 million titles; 70,000 new titles are added to the data base each year, and all are for sale in published form or on microfiche. The NTIS also sells technical-information products such as computer software, and it handles the licensing of government-owned patents (patented inventions created through government research).

Economic Development Administration

The Economic Development Administration (EDA), established in 1965, was created to generate new jobs, to help protect existing jobs, and to stimulate commercial and industrial growth in economically distressed areas of the United States. The EDA assists rural and urban areas of the nation that are experiencing high unemployment, low income, or sudden and severe economic distress. It awards grants to communities in economically depressed areas to provide jobs and to strengthen local tax bases through growth in industry and commerce. EDA grants are usually allocated to help build public facilities, such as access roads, water and sewer lines, port and airport terminals, and industrial parks. These projects will provide the basic foundation necessary for economic growth and increase the potential for creating permanent jobs. In 1988, the EDA awarded 199 grants for a total of $120.1 million in financial assistance for public works.

The EDA operates a technical-assistance program to help local communities develop available resources. This program also provides grants to determine the economic feasibility of various job-producing projects and strategies. The EDA supports projects in rural America that help small farmers survive by strengthening cooperatives, that identify alternative-employment opportunities, and that diversify rural economies.

Minority Business Development Agency

The Minority Business Development Agency (MBDA), established in 1969 when President Richard Nixon signed Executive Order 11458, was created specifically to foster the establishment and growth of minority-owned businesses in America. The MBDA provides assistance to socially or economically disadvantaged individuals who own or wish to start a business. Such people include blacks, Spanish-speaking Americans, Native Americans, Eskimos, Aleuts, Asian Americans, and Asian Indians.

Ground is broken in 1989 for Hancock Airpark, a 125-acre commercial and industrial park near Syracuse, New York, funded by the Economic Development Administration (EDA). The EDA awards grants to communities in economically depressed areas to provide jobs and to encourage growth in local industry and commerce. The EDA grants are usually used to help build public facilities such as industrial parks, water and sewer lines, and transportation terminals.

The MBDA helps minority businesses become more competitive by providing funds for a network of approximately 100 Minority Business Development Centers located throughout the country. These centers—operated by profit and nonprofit organizations, state or local governments, or educational institutions—are staffed by business specialists who have the knowledge and practical experience needed to run successful, profitable businesses. They provide minority entrepreneurs (people who organize, manage, and assume the risk of a business) with management and technical assistance to enable them to start, expand, or manage their businesses. The MBDA also helps federal, state, and local government agencies—as well as major corporations—increase their purchases from minority-owned firms. By the late 1980s there were more than 800,000 minority-owned firms in the United States, up from an estimated 100,000 in 1969, when the MBDA was created. Along with the U.S. Small Business Administration, the MBDA also cosponsors Minority Enterprise Development Week (MED Week), an annual celebration to honor the contributions of America's minority entrepreneurs and those individuals and organizations that actively support minority business development. During MED Week, the first full week in October, activities include workshops and seminars on topics of interest to minority entrepreneurs, a marketplace where

A Korean-American greengrocer arranges his merchandise. The Minority Business Development Administration helps minority businesses become more competitive by providing experienced and knowledgeable business experts to advise minority entrepreneurs.

public- and private-sector buyers meet with minority vendors, and an awards banquet to honor outstanding minority entrepreneurs and their advocates.

MBDA headquarters are located in Washington, D.C., where all activities are planned and developed. The MBDA has six regional offices—in Atlanta, Chicago, Dallas, New York, San Francisco, and Washington, D.C.—where staff members oversee assistance services in multistate regions.

International Trade Administration

Created in 1980 in response to the highly charged trade competition in world markets, the International Trade Administration (ITA) is the division most closely identified with the department's primary mission: to foster and develop commerce and industry in the United States. The ITA endeavors to promote world trade and to strengthen the U.S. position in international trade and investment. International trade has become an increasingly important factor in the U.S. economy: One in eight jobs in manufacturing depends on exports, and one in four farm acres are planted for export. The ITA is organized into four divisions: Trade Development, U.S. and Foreign Commercial Service, International Economic Policy, and Import Administration.

Trade Development's mission is to assess and improve U.S. industrial competitiveness in the global economy. Through cooperation with U.S. industry, it identifies trade, financial, and investment opportunities for U.S. businesses and service industries. It also develops trade policies and initiatives to increase exports and reduce or remove barriers that affect the ability of U.S. firms to capitalize on expanded market opportunities in the world economy.

Trade Development's activities are organized into seven industry sectors: aerospace; automotive affairs and consumer goods; basic industries, such as chemicals, wood and paper products, and coal; capital goods and international construction; science and electronics; services; and textiles and apparel. Each provides industry with a central point of contact in the Department of Commerce. For example, the aerospace sector office assists the U.S. aerospace industry in maintaining and expanding its contribution to U.S. trade. In 1988, the office released a study entitled "Competitive Assessment of the U.S. Helicopter Industry," which focused on the challenges facing the helicopter industry and the need for the industry to restructure to meet a changing domestic market at a time when the export market remained strong.

Through its U.S. and Foreign Commercial Service (US&FCS), the ITA helps small- and medium-sized businesses market their goods abroad. With offices in 64 cities in the United States and in 66 foreign countries, US&FCS

RECEPTION - INFORMATION
РЕЦЕПЦИЯ - ИНФОРМАЦИЯ

International Trade Administration (ITA) officials meet with representatives of the Soviet Union at the Soviet International Food Processing Equipment Trade Show in 1986, which marked the resumption of formal U.S. trade promotion in the Soviet Union. The ITA endeavors to strengthen the U.S. position in international trade.

trade specialists and foreign commercial experts—the eyes and the ears of the ITA—guide U.S. firms through all stages of the export transaction, from identifying products with potential for export to assisting the firms in promoting them abroad. For example, foreign commercial officers are gathering information on the European Economic Community's plan to become an integrated common market in 1992 and alerting U.S. firms to the obstacles and opportunities that European market integration will present. US&FCS representatives also gather commercial information, sponsor trade exhibitions, and line up foreign sales representatives for U.S. products.

The US&FCS sponsors EXPORT NOW!, a nationwide public-awareness campaign designed to encourage smaller companies to test their products in world markets. In 1988, US&FCS district-office trade specialists arranged 3,200 seminars that helped hundreds of first-time exporters find overseas markets.

The International Economic Policy (IEP) division of the ITA develops and implements policy concerning U.S. international trade, investment, and commercial relations. The IEP identifies foreign barriers to trade and commercial opportunities in the world marketplace. The IEP is organized by country, and through its country desks it counsels U.S. businesses on how to conduct business abroad. For example, a U.S. toy manufacturer that wanted to export its goods to Eastern Europe could receive expert advice from the country desks specializing in Poland, Czechoslovakia, and Hungary.

The IEP also participates in international trade negotiations. For example, it assisted in drafting the U.S.-Canada Free Trade Agreement and began an outreach program to inform U.S. businesses about the provisions and implications of the agreement.

The ITA's Import Administration investigates complaints of "dumping," that is, charges that foreign goods are being sold in the United States at less than fair market value in order to undercut domestic producers. The Import Administration is also responsible for determining whether foreign governments are subsidizing exports to this country. These practices are illegal under U.S. law and the General Agreement on Tariffs and Trade (GATT).

Bureau of Export Administration

The Bureau of Export Administration (BXA) was created in 1987 to establish policy for the export of certain commodities and high-technology products that could harm U.S. national security or enhance the military capabilities of potential adversaries. For example, computers and other high-technology equipment intended for sale to the Soviet Union or Eastern European countries must be licensed for sale and export by the bureau. The BXA encourages voluntary compliance with export control laws but is empowered to employ criminal and administrative sanctions against violators.

U.S. Travel and Tourism Administration

More than 30 million foreign visitors enter the United States every year, providing jobs and bringing billions of dollars into the American economy. The United States Travel and Tourism Administration (USTTA), the national tourism office, was established in 1981 to expand export earnings and job opportunities by promoting business and pleasure travel to the United States.

Through its 10 marketing offices in Toronto, Mexico City, Tokyo, Sydney, London, Paris, Frankfurt, Amsterdam, Milan, and Miami (for South America), the USTTA develops marketing programs to attract visitors. Extensive

Using the dramatic nighttime Seattle skyline as a backdrop, Japanese tourists record their visit to the United States with a photograph. The United States Travel and Tourism Administration promotes business and pleasure travel to the United States to increase export earnings and job opportunities for Americans.

cooperative print and television advertising programs are used to encourage foreign travel agents and tour operators to sell U.S. destinations to their clients and to encourage prospective travelers to select the United States as their travel destination.

The USTTA also persuades international associations to choose U.S. locations for future congresses and meetings. For example, the USTTA assisted in the successful effort promoting the United States as the site for the 1994 World Cup soccer tournament. The World Cup is expected to attract 3 million spectators—more than half of them foreign visitors. Tourism revenues from this event are expected to exceed $1.5 billion.

The USTTA provides multilingual receptionists capable of speaking 29 languages at 12 major U.S. international airports. The receptionists provide services such as acting as interpreters for arriving international tourists who require assistance with U.S. entry formalities.

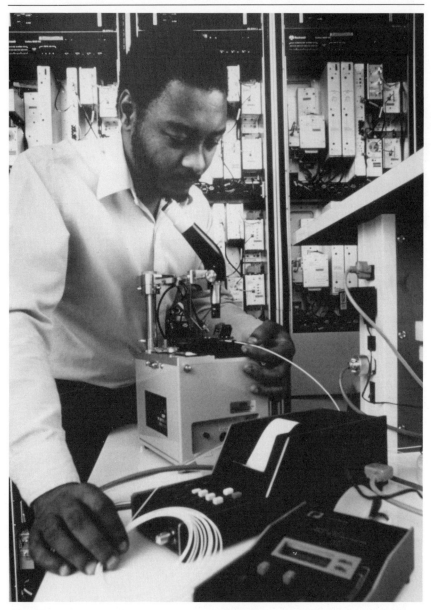

An MCI Communications Corporation technician uses a laser to splice fiber-optic telephone cables. The Department of Commerce provides many services to U.S. industries, including developing technologies that improve communications.

FIVE

The Challenge of the 21st Century

The Department of Commerce has been in partnership with American business for more than 75 years. It provides business with basic economic research data necessary for it to make sound decisions on industrial growth. This partnership has resulted in innovative programs and scientific break-throughs in manufacturing, transportation, communications, measurement, and materials, which continue to ensure the United States a leadership role in the international marketplace.

The Department of Commerce is at the forefront of the technological revolution ushering in the 21st century, providing many indispensable services in our modern, technology-driven society. Through offices in major U.S. cities and in 66 foreign countries, the department develops international trade opportunities and administers legislation that helps U.S. industry and labor counter unfair foreign-trade practices. By promoting the increased use of science and technology in the development of U.S. industrial capacity and the production of consumer goods, the department is an important cornerstone of the U.S. economy, supporting America's economic competitiveness in world markets.

The department's laboratories and research facilities have produced a vast array of new products and technologies that are revolutionizing the way we live and work:

- New materials, such as high-performance composites (synthetics), whose strength, stiffness, corrosion resistance, and design flexibility are changing manufacturing processes and form the basis for important new industries.
- Sensitive measurement techniques to monitor and control the manufacture of products from microorganisms and animal and plant cells.
- Bioengineering processes that are yielding a host of valuable new drugs, chemicals, and other commercially important substances.
- Basic research in optics and light-wave technology, which is, even today, paving the way for advanced computer and communications systems.

America's economic future is dependent on many factors: human innovation and creativity; excellence in product design and manufacturing efficiency; a good market sense and sales acumen. In each of these critical areas, the Department of Commerce plays an important role.

Patents and trademarks, which are registered with the Department of Commerce, encourage inventors, businessmen, and entrepreneurs to invent and create by assuring them that their work will not be pirated by others and that they will reap the rewards of their own efforts. Development of industrial robots and research in automated manufacturing by the National Institute of Standards and Technology (NIST) is providing the critical base of engineering knowledge and experience necessary for American industry to compete with the Japanese and others in the manufacturing environment of the future. And detailed statistics gathered by Commerce Department agencies, which document virtually every aspect of our economy and foreign trade as well, provide American businesses with essential information for spotting important trends and for planning effective marketing campaigns.

As the 21st century approaches, several issues are emerging in the press, and in the public mind, that have major implications for the future of the United States and the world. Significant growth in nonmanufacturing sectors, first noted by a Commerce Department survey in the 1920s, has continued to the present day—with profound effects on the American way of life, communities, educational requirements for workers, and job opportunities. Many communities that had once benefited by the rise of manufacturing and heavy industry, such as Youngstown, Ohio (steel), and Flint, Michigan (automobiles), have

*One of the more than 3,000 employees being laid off at a General Motors
plant in Flint, Michigan, uses his shop apron as a banner on the final day of
the plant's operation in 1987. Assisting the nation in adapting to an economy
dominated by service industries and new technologies rather than heavy
manufacturing presents one of the many challenges facing the Department of
Commerce as the 21st century approaches.*

fallen into decline. At the same time, other communities, such as Atlanta, that perhaps were better able to seize opportunities as commercial service and retail centers, have thrived. Workers who have been unable to meet the changing educational requirements and skill levels of the now-dominant service economy have suffered as many new and exciting opportunities have been created, especially those related to applications of science and technology.

The threat to the earth's environment posed by the depletion of atmospheric ozone, the "greenhouse effect," air and water pollution, and destruction of wildlife habitats, are all matters of growing concern. With a 1990 budget of $1.2 billion, a technical staff including 2,200 oceanographers, meteorologists, and other scientists, a fleet of 23 ships, a small squadron of aircraft, and a half dozen satellites in orbit, the Commerce Department's National Oceanic and Atmospheric Administration (NOAA) is uniquely capable of addressing some of the most troublesome global environmental issues. Furthermore, in addition to these impressive physical resources, NOAA's responsibilities surely complement—if not rival—those of the Environmental Protection Agency in the area of environmental sciences research.

Political changes in the Soviet Union and Eastern Europe, which have started a movement toward greater personal freedom and the development of market-based economies, could profoundly alter political and economic relationships between the Communist world and the West. American business has long eyed the Soviet Union and Eastern Europe as representing a vast market characterized by enormous and unsatisfied consumer demand. However, aside from a few highly visible point ventures such as McDonald's fast-food franchise in Moscow and Pepsi Cola's entry into the Soviet market in the 1970s, American business has been discouraged by the Soviet bureaucracy, the inability to convert the ruble to dollars, and, especially, political uncertainties. Although these factors still stand as major impediments, the Department of Commerce is receiving an increasing number of queries and requests for assistance from American businesses excited by the promise of *glasnost* and *perestroika*—the new regime of openness and restructuring—that has raised expectations in both the East and West.

Until the 1980s, tourism among the Soviet Union, Eastern Europe, and the United States had been a virtual one-way street. Americans have traveled in increasing numbers to the Communist East, but relatively few, other than officials or business travelers, from the Communist nations have visited the United States. Now, however, with the general relaxation in East-West tensions and with the loosening of travel restrictions imposed by their

A West Berliner smashes a sledgehammer into the Berlin Wall in November 1989. After the political changes that swept through Eastern Europe and the Soviet Union opened up new business opportunities, the Department of Commerce received many requests for assistance from American businesses seeking to market their goods in those areas.

governments on citizens of the Eastern bloc, America's tourism industry stands to benefit. The U.S. Travel and Tourism Administration is already being presented with a new tourist market of immense potential, one that will require development of a unique marketing and sales approach.

With respect to these and related issues, it seems certain that the Department of Commerce will be called on to engage its resources in responding to new opportunities and the challenges they represent. In the final analysis, success of the central mission of the Department of Commerce— promoting the nation's international trade and economic growth—will determine the quality of American life in the 21st century. For this reason, the department has undertaken a number of special projects designed to help maintain and expand America's competitive edge in the global marketplace.

A computer-controlled robot stacks cartons of film on pallets at the Eastman Kodak Company in Rochester, New York. To stimulate the development of U.S. industrial capacity and to promote the production of consumer goods, the Department of Commerce encourages U.S. businesses to adopt advanced technologies such as robotics.

For example, NIST is supporting three new regional manufacturing technology centers, designed to assist small- and medium-sized industry in utilizing sophisticated robotics and other recent dramatic advances in manufacturing technology. These include the Cleveland Advanced Manufacturing Program, located on the campus of Cuyahoga Community College, Cleveland, Ohio; the Northeast Manufacturing Center, established in collaboration with Rensselaer Polytechnic Institute, Troy, New York; and the South Carolina Technology Transfer Cooperative, established by the University of South Carolina and the state's technical-college system.

Workers and plant managers may view state-of-the-art manufacturing equipment and techniques at the centers and participate in special training activities. The Commerce Department's Automated Manufacturing Research Facility—the so-called experimental factory of the future—will be used by the manufacturing centers as a primary source of new ideas and of demonstration equipment and technologies.

Another Department of Commerce facility, dedicated in January 1989, will give U.S. industry prime access to one of the key tools of modern materials science. The Cold Neutron Research Facility (CNRF), located in Gaithersburg, Maryland, uses beams of neutrons, produced by nuclear research reactors, to study the arrangements and interactions of atoms in various materials. Neutrons are highly penetrating, which makes it possible to probe deep within materials, to identify cracks, voids, and other submicroscopic structures. Because of their special properties "cold" neutrons—refrigerated to -415 degrees Fahrenheit—have greatly extended neutron research. Practical applications of this research area include development of high-temperature superconductors, which can significantly improve the efficiency of electrical equipment and of new catalytic materials for use in oil refining and the production of special chemicals. Cold neutron research also permits study of materials critical to advances in the semiconductor industry.

The Department of Commerce has been in partnership with American business during one of history's most turbulent and creative eras. The rapid pace of change in the 20th century and the transforming effect of science and technology on everyday life were, in many cases, encouraged and nurtured by the department. Just as the development of radio and aviation and the popularization of the automobile owe much to the policies and programs of the Department of Commerce in its early years, so, too, will the agency, as the 21st century approaches, strongly influence the future of America's communications industry, the quality of our natural environment, and the products of the nation's great and varied scientific enterprise.

Department of Commerce

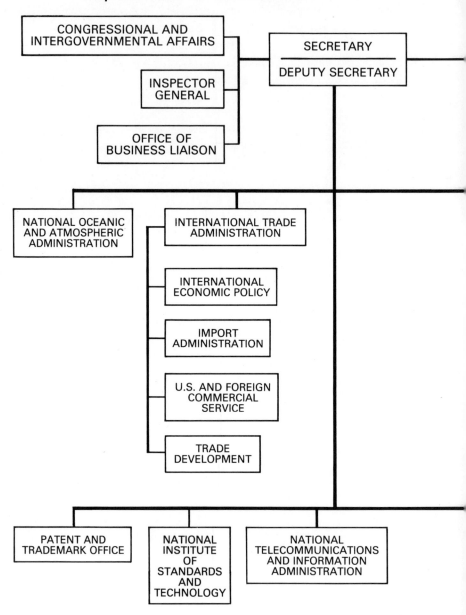

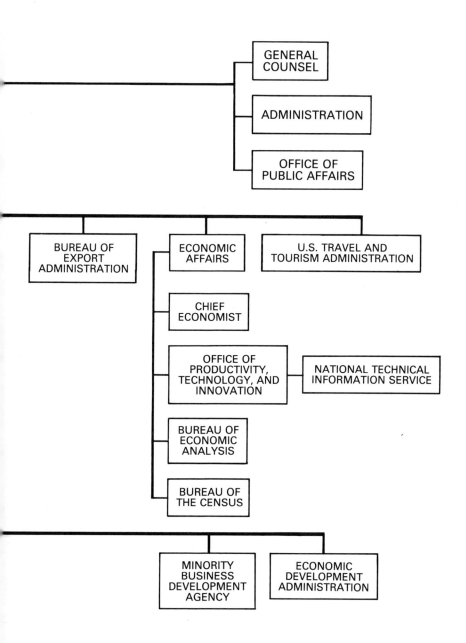

GENERAL
COUNSEL

ADMINISTRATION

OFFICE OF
PUBLIC AFFAIRS

BUREAU OF
EXPORT
ADMINISTRATION

ECONOMIC
AFFAIRS

U.S. TRAVEL AND
TOURISM ADMINISTRATION

CHIEF
ECONOMIST

OFFICE OF
PRODUCTIVITY,
TECHNOLOGY, AND
INNOVATION

NATIONAL TECHNICAL
INFORMATION SERVICE

BUREAU OF
ECONOMIC
ANALYSIS

BUREAU OF
THE CENSUS

MINORITY
BUSINESS
DEVELOPMENT
AGENCY

ECONOMIC
DEVELOPMENT
ADMINISTRATION

GLOSSARY

Articles of Confederation and Perpetual Union   The first constitution by which the United States was governed from 1781 until the ratification of the present Constitution in 1789.

Balance of payments   The amount of money that flows in and out of a country, including the value of imports and exports, loans and investments, foreign aid, and income from tourism.

Census   A periodic government enumeration of the population. The Bureau of the Census conducts a count of the total population of the United States every 10 years.

Commerce   The buying and selling of commodities, transportation and commercial intercourse, and the transmission of radio, television, and telephonic and telegraphic messages.

Commerce clause   The clause of the Constitution that gives Congress the power to regulate all business activities affecting more than one state and that also prohibits states from discriminating against business activities of other nations or states.

Entrepreneur   A person who plans, organizes, manages, and owns a business and assumes the risks of the enterprise.

European Economic Community (EEC)   An economic alliance established in 1958 by Belgium, France, Italy, Luxembourg, the Netherlands, and West Germany (and later joined by the United Kingdom, Ireland, Denmark, Greece, Spain, and Portugal) to adopt common import duties and expedite trade among the member nations.

General Agreement on Tariffs and Trade (GATT)   An international treaty that liberalizes trade between the nearly 90 signatory nations by reducing tariffs and other trade barriers and that provides a forum for the settlement of international trade disputes.

Gross national product (GNP)   The total market value of all final goods and services produced in a country in a given period of time (usually one year).

Patent An exclusive right granted by the U.S. government to an inventor to make, use, license, or sell for 17 years a new device, process, material, or other innovation.

Standard A criterion established by an authority as a rule for the measure of quantity, weight, extent, value, or quality.

Tariff A charge imposed by a government on imported products to raise money and to protect domestic industries.

Trademark A distinguishing symbol, device, or term used in connection with a product or service and whose exclusive use is legally reserved for its owner.

Trust An illegal combination of companies whose stock is controlled by a board of trustees for the purpose of controlling prices and eliminating competition.

SELECTED REFERENCES

Beard, Charles A. *An Economic Interpretation of the Constitution of the United States*. New York: Macmillan, 1935.

Cochrane, Rexmond C. *Measures for Progress, A History of the National Bureau of Standards*. Washington, DC: U.S. Department of Commerce, 1966.

Eckler, A. Ross. *The Bureau of the Census*. New York: Praeger, 1972.

Hawley, Ellis W., ed. *Herbert Hoover as Secretary of State: Studies in New Era Thought and Practice*. Iowa City: University of Iowa Press, 1981.

Miller, Arthur R., and Michael H. Davis. *Intellectual Property: Patents, Trademarks, and Copyrights*. St. Paul, MN: West Publishing Co., 1983.

U.S. Department of Commerce. *Annual Report of the Secretary of Commerce*. Washington, DC: U.S. Government Printing Office, 1988.

————. *From Lighthouses to Laserbeams: A History of the Department of Commerce*. Washington, DC: U.S. Government Printing Office, 1988.

————. International Trade Administration. *United States Trade Performance in 1988*. Washington, DC: U.S. Government Printing Office, 1989.

————. National Institute of Standards and Technology. *Facilities*. Washington, DC: U.S. Government Printing Office, 1988.

————. Patent and Trademark Office. *General Information Concerning Patents*. Washington, DC: U.S. Government Printing Office, 1989.

Whitnah, Donald R., ed. *Government Agencies*. The Greenwood Encyclopedia of American Institutions. Westport, CT: Greenwood Press, 1983.

INDEX

First Bank of the United
States, 26
Fisheries, Bureau of, 32, 37, 39,
47, 53, 63
Flint, Michigan, 88
Ford, Henry, 70
Foreign Affairs, Department of,
26
Foreign and Domestic Com-
merce, Bureau of, 34, 37, 41,
45, 47, 50
Franklin, Benjamin, 61

Gaithersburg, Maryland, 93
Gandhi, Rajiv, 53
General Agreement on Tariffs
and Trade (GATT), 50, 84
General Counsel, Office of
(OGC), 58
General Weather Service, 16
Gorbachev, Mikhail, 53
Grant, Ulysses S., 63
Great Depression, 44

Hamilton, Alexander, 22–23, 26
Harding, Warren G., 39, 43
Herbert Clark Hoover Building,
57
Hodges, Luther H., 50
Hoover, Herbert, 39, 41, 43–44,
74
House of Representatives, U.S.,
32, 77

Immigration, Bureau of, 31
Industrial Commission, U.S.,
31
Industrial Revolution, 17
Inspector General, Office of, 59
Interior, Department of the, 47,
63, 70
International Trade, Office of,
48
International Trade Adminis-
tration (ITA), 60, 82–84
Interstate Highway Act, 50

Jefferson, Thomas, 32, 61, 63
Justice Department, 26

Kennedy, John F., 50, 74
Korean War, 50

Labor, Bureau of, 32, 35, 37
Labor, Department of, 32, 35
Lighthouse Board, 32
Lighthouses, Bureau of, 37, 38,
47
London, England, 50
Lusitania, 39

McKinley, William, 31
Madison, James, 22, 23
Magnuson Act, 63
Manufactures, Bureau of, 34
Marconi, Guglielmo, 70
Maritime Administration, 50, 51
Metcalf, Victor H., 32
Mexico, 28
Minority Business Development
Agency (MBDA), 53, 60, 79–
81
Morris, Gouverneur, 24–25
Mount Vernon Conference, 22

Nagel, Charles, 32
National Aeronautics and
Space Administration
(NASA), 60, 62
National Defense Reserve
Fleet, 51
National Environmental Satel-
lite Data and Information
Service, 61, 64
National Fire Prevention and
Control Administration, 53
National Hurricane Research
Project, 62
National Industrial Recovery
Act, 46, 47
National Institute of Standards
and Technology (NIST), 55,
60, 65–68, 88, 92

National Inventors Council, 48
National Marine Fisheries Service, 55, 61, 63
National Oceanic and Atmospheric Administration (NOAA), 52, 60–65, 90
National Ocean Service, 53, 61, 63
National Recovery Administration (NRA), 46
National Science Foundation, 60
National Technical Information Service (NTIS), 48, 74
National Telecommunications and Information Administration (NTIA), 60, 68–69
National Weather Service, 61
Navigation, Bureau of, 31, 37
New Deal, 45
New Industrial Day, The (Redfield), 37
New Orleans, Louisiana, 38
New York City, 38
Nexrad, 63
Nixon, Richard M., 52, 53, 79
Northeast Manufacturing Center, 92

Oceanic and Atmospheric Research, Office of, 61, 65

Pacific Ocean, 28
Panama Canal, 18
Patent and Trademark Office (PTO), 60, 69–73
Philadelphia, Pennsylvania, 15, 24
Potomac River, 22
Productivity, Technology, and Innovation, Office of (OPTI), 74, 78
Public Affairs, Office of, 59
Public Roads, Bureau of, 50

Randolph, Edmund, 23
Reagan, Ronald, 53

Redfield, William C., 37, 39
Rensselaer Polytechnic Institute, 92
Report on Manufactures, 26
Roosevelt, Franklin D., 45–47
Roosevelt, Theodore, 17, 31, 32
Roper, Daniel C., 45

St. Louis, Missouri, 38
San Francisco, California, 38
Schecter Poultry Corp. v. U.S., 47
Seattle, Washington, 38
Senate, U.S., 57
Shays, Daniel, 24
Shays's Rebellion, 23
Sherman Antitrust Act of 1890, 31
Small Business Administration, 81
South Carolina Technology Transfer Cooperative, 92
Soviet Union, 48, 53, 90
Standards, Bureau of, 32, 37, 48, 50, 55, 65
Stans, Maurice, 52
State, Department of, 26, 47, 70
Statistics, Bureau of, 32
Steamboat Inspection Service, 16, 32, 37
Straus, Oscar S., 18, 32, 39
Supreme Court, U.S., 47

Taft, William Howard, 17, 31, 35
Tesla, Nikola, 70
Transportation, Department of, 50
Transportation, Office of, 50
Travel and Tourism Administration, 51, 60, 84–85, 90
Treasury, Department of the, 26, 32, 47, 65

U.S.-Canada Free Trade Agreement (FTA), 58

PICTURE CREDITS

Robert J. Griffin, Jr., public affairs specialist at the Department of Energy, is a member of the National Press Club and the Government Information Organization. Griffin is the author of numerous magazine articles and public information materials, including the award-winning publications *Energy Conservation: Understanding and Activities for Young People* and *What About Metric?*

Arthur M. Schlesinger, jr., served in the White House as special assistant to Presidents Kennedy and Johnson. He is the author of numerous acclaimed works in American history and twice has been awarded the Pulitzer Prize. He taught history at Harvard College for many years and is currently Albert Schweitzer Professor of the Humanities at the City College of New York.